# Preparing Future Faculty in the Humanities and Social Sciences

## A Guide for Change

*Jerry G. Gaff*
*Anne S. Pruitt-Logan*
*Leslie B. Sims*
*Daniel D. Denecke*
*And Program Participants*

Council of Graduate Schools
Association of American Colleges and Universities

Washington, DC 2003

This material is based upon work supported by The Atlantic Philanthropies.


Any opinions, findings, and conclusions or recommendations expressed in this material are those of the author(s) and do not necessarily reflect the views of The Atlantic Philanthropies.

# Table of Contents

# Preface

While President of the Council of Graduate Schools, Jules LaPidus character-
ized the traditional role of doctoral education in the research university as one
designed to "...produce chemists, historians, mathematicians, and individuals
in a host of other disciplines; it is not to prepare people for any specific job or
career." (1995, p.35) Further, he noted, "There is a basic flaw in this approach,
. . . in that students educated in this way are quite likely to perceive their graduate experience as a model for their careers and to expect to continue, after the
Ph.D., doing much the same kind of thing they did as graduate students." In
reality, the work of most faculty members is quite different from the narrowly
specialized research focus of doctoral education.

The tradition that LaPidus critiqued still shapes much of doctoral education. But there is increased activity that promises to break this mold, so that
doctoral students who aspire to the professoriate can learn about the work that
faculty members actually do.

For nearly a decade, the Preparing Future Faculty (PFF) program has cultivated a new vision of the preparation of college and university faculty. This
new vision identifies teaching, research, and service as the three expectations
for faculty at most institutions of higher learning and asserts that doctoral students planning to join the faculty should begin learning about each of these
elements of the academic profession prior to earning the degree. This new
vision holds that students should gain experience with faculty roles in both
their home institutions and institutions not usually involved in doctoral education, e.g., liberal arts and community colleges and master's institutions.

The decade-long accomplishments of PFF have been possible thanks to a remarkably successful collaboration between two Washington-based educational associations: The Council of Graduate Schools (CGS), whose mission is to enhance graduate education, and the Association of American Colleges and Universities (AAC&U), whose mission is to advance undergraduate liberal education. These two organizations co-sponsored PFF partnerships between the "producers" (the universities that educate prospective faculty) and the "consumers" (those institutions that employ them). As a result of these efforts, PFF is now recognized as a valuable contribution to doctoral education.

This volume describes PFF programs in the social sciences and humanities and documents their feasibility—indeed, their desirability. It is a companion to Preparing Future Faculty in the Sciences and Mathematics: A Guide for Change (2002), which illustrates the programs and viability of PFF in those disciplines. This volume also builds on the earlier publication Building the Faculty We Need: Colleges and Universities Working Together (2000), which summarizes the value and benefits of PFF programs operated by graduate schools.

In particular, this report summarizes the lessons learned in a three-year project called "Shaping the Preparation of Future Humanities and Social Science Faculty." The project featured leadership by six disciplinary societies: American Historical Association, American Political Science Association, American Psychological Association, American Sociological Association, National Communication Association, and National Council of Teachers of English. These societies selected departments in their disciplines to develop programs that implemented the PFF vision.

This project culminates a line of work begun in 1993 with two grants from The Pew Charitable Trusts to AAC&U in partnership with CGS to assist graduate schools, first to create and then to institutionalize PFF programs. In 1998, we began forming partnerships with disciplinary societies. The National Science Foundation provided support for the period 1998-2002 to engage disciplinary societies in chemistry, computer science, life sciences, mathematics, and physics and to support departments in developing PFF programs in their fields. The project that is the subject of this book was funded from 1999 to 2002 by The Atlantic Philanthropies, which provided grants to six disciplinary societies to develop PFF programs in academic departments in their discipline. Together, departments and societies in 11 disciplines have cultivated PFF programs in 44 departments that previously had not developed a PFF program.

This book is organized into six sections: the vision and its rationale, strategies for introducing PFF programs, illustrative content of the programs, activities of the societies and reflections of their executives, information about the outcomes, and challenges for the future. These sections identify actions that faculty members, administrators, and others who care about the effectiveness of faculty members can take to prepare the next generation of professors for important and challenging careers. We hope that information about this new approach to preparing doctoral students for academic careers will encourage additional social science and humanities departments to pursue their own innovations.

The primary audiences for this publication are faculty members, academic administrators, graduate students, and others interested in the quality and preparation of college and university faculty. Others who might be interested include boards of trustees, state and national policy makers, leaders of educational associations, providers of graduate fellowships, and, in fact, anyone interested in improving the quality of graduate and undergraduate education.

We are privileged to have been able to work on this project with so many thoughtful, energetic, and committed colleagues, who are taking the lead in preparing our successor generation for the academy. These individuals contributed to the success of this project and to the preparation of this report. Foremost are the PFF leaders who managed the work within the disciplinary societies that partnered with PFF:

▲ Paul Bodmer, Associate Executive Director, National Council of Teachers of English;

▲ Noralee Frankel, Assistant Director, Women, Minorities, and Teaching, American Historical Association;

▲ Carla Howery, Deputy Executive Officer, American Sociological Association;

▲ Sheilah Mann, Director, Education and Professional Development, American Political Science Association;

▲ Sherwyn Morreale, Associate Director, National Communication Association; and

▲ Paul D. Nelson, Executive Director, Education Directorate, American Psychological Association.

The twenty-five academic departments that were selected to participate in this program are listed in the Appendix, along with their faculty leaders. Those faculty leaders helped their colleagues design new PFF programs, recruited faculty members and students in their disciplines, and implemented the programs. The ideas and information they shared about their efforts to establish the PFF programs constitute the heart of this volume.

Faculty members and academic administrators at partner campuses were pivotal to the operation of these PFF programs, and many of their comments appear in this volume. The partner institutions provided PFF graduate students with insights about faculty and student life on their campuses. These institutions also are listed in Appendix II. Graduate students who decided to take a chance by enrolling in an innovative program, sometimes against the advice of their research advisors, were also essential to the success of these programs, and their experiences and judgments are included throughout this book.

Several colleagues at CGS and AAC&U deserve special mention for providing valuable assistance throughout this project: at CGS, Debra Stewart, president; Leslie Sims, senior scholar in residence and director of external grants programs; and Daniel Denecke, PFF program manager; and at AAC&U, Carol Geary Schneider, president; Alma Clayton-Pedersen, vice president for education and institutional renewal; and Charles Bashara, associate director of PFF. Two individuals who left before this publication was completed but who made significant contributions to the project deserve our acknowledgement. Richard Weibl served as PFF program manager at AAC&U for the first two years of the project and was instrumental in its success, as was Tracie Fellers, PFF program manager at CGS.

For its generous support of this project, we are grateful to The Atlantic Philanthropies. We appreciate the support of the AP staff, especially Theodore Hullar, our program officer, who was extremely helpful as we implemented this large, complex, collaborative project.

This initiative in the social sciences and humanities was built on two earlier university-wide PFF projects funded by The Pew Charitable Trusts, with outstanding leadership from Ellen Wert, program officer. During most of the life of this project, we benefited from the leadership and consultation with participants in those two previous initiatives. In addition, a parallel project funded by the National Science Foundation (NSF) focused on developing PFF programs in the natural sciences and mathematics. This parallel project enjoyed strong continuing leadership from Myles Boylan, NSF program officer, and Norman Fortenberry, director, NSF Division of Undergraduate Education, Directorate for Education and Human Resources. Each of these previous and parallel initiatives enriched the current project.

A collaborative writing effort produced this publication. PFF program directors (familiarly known as "cluster leaders") at the doctoral-granting institutions involved in the project responded to a number of questions posed by the national PFF staff and society executives. The disciplinary society executives provided information about activities in their individual disciplines and held a focus group discussion on lessons learned. The disciplinary society executives and our colleagues at CGS and AAC&U reviewed drafts of this volume.

To all who contributed, we are grateful.

Anne S. Pruitt-Logan,
Scholar in Residence at CGS,
Principal Investigator

Jerry G. Gaff, Senior Scholar at AAC&U,
Co-Principal Investigator

Washington, DC
January 2003

# Acknowledgements

In their preface, Anne Pruitt-Logan and Jerry Gaff offer a rich account of the history that provides the context for the most recent phase of the PFF program—broadening the graduate preparation of students in the humanities and social sciences who aspire to academic careers. Jerry Gaff was the director of PFF at its inception in 1993, and he and co-director Anne Pruitt-Logan are largely responsible for its success. We are grateful to them for the manuscript that served as the basis for final revisions and editing that resulted in the present volume–only the most recent of a large number of publications, presentations, and other contributions that they have made to the PFF initiative. Our most sincere thanks go to Anita Blumenthal for her helpful editing of the manuscript and to Ann Kammerer for her excellent design and layout for this volume. We must also thank our collaborators in the humanities and social science disciplinary societies. All of us worked hard to accurately document the experiences of those involved in these campus cluster projects, to show the benefits for those who participated, and to provide a useful guide to those wishing to establish their own programs to prepare future faculty.

Leslie B. Sims, Senior Scholar in Residence, CGS

Daniel D. Denecke, PFF Program Manager, CGS

Washington, DC
January 2003

# Chapter 1

# A New Vision of Doctoral Preparation

*Not only has the PFF program taught me "how" to become a professor, it has also assured me that this is the profession for me.*
——Graduate Student in Communication, Indiana University

Graduate education in the United States is a large and enormously successful enterprise, attracting students from nearly every country in the world, and serving as a major source of research and innovation that supports economic development and enhances the quality of life. Yet, like any successful endeavor, there is room for improvement, and many studies and reports point to changes that would make graduate education more responsive to the needs of students and of society.

The Preparing Future Faculty program, known familiarly as PFF, sets forth a new vision of doctoral preparation for future faculty. This PFF program in the humanities and social sciences involved disciplinary societies in communication, English, history, political science, psychology, and sociology. These societies selected departments in their discipline to participate in a collaborative effort to better prepare doctoral students for the whole range of expectations of faculty in a variety of educational institutions. This volume describes these efforts and presents information to help those who wish to benefit from the lessons learned from this project.

The hallmark of a doctoral degree has always been and remains the requirement to demonstrate mastery of the field and to apply that knowledge to conduct original research that expands the knowledge base of the discipline. After World War II, a social compact evolved among government, business, and education that ceded to universities a major responsibility for conducting research in the nation's interest. An array of federal agencies was established to fund this work and to ensure that the United States maintained its leadership position. The great majority of this research is conducted as part of graduate, particularly doctoral, education. As a consequence, research has become the dominant or nearly exclusive requirement for the Ph.D. degree, and graduates are well prepared for research-related careers. In addition, all employers expect competencies in other areas, but preparation for such areas is seldom part of doctoral programs.

Approximately 50 percent of doctoral graduates pursue academic careers (Hoffer, Dugoni, Sanderson, Sederstrom, Welch, Guzmon-Barron, Brown 2002). However, only 25 percent of faculty positions (32 percent of full-time positions) are at research universities (Berger, Kirschstein, and Rowe 2001). Thus, only about one-third of doctoral graduates can expect to become faculty members at research universities similar to their graduate institution, where research is the predominant requirement for earning tenure. Approximately 75 percent of faculty positions are in other types of institutions, where teaching and professional and community service roles are of equal or greater importance. Doctoral programs seldom adequately prepare students for the realities of faculty life, particularly in these different sorts of institutions. Indeed, even research universities increasingly demand that faculty be attentive to their teaching and service roles. Better preparation for academic careers includes understanding the missions, faculty roles and rewards, and academic culture of the various institutions. Preparation should also allow students to experience the full range of roles faculty play in these institutions and to develop the skills that will allow them to compete for and succeed in faculty positions.

Although a significant fraction of graduate students have teaching assignments sometime during their doctoral program, too often these are not structured experiences that prepare graduates to deal with the assessment and different types of student learning, the pedagogy of the discipline, curricular innovations, the impact of technology on education, or the variety of teaching styles that may be helpful with students from different racial, ethnic, or cultural backgrounds. Even less common are activities relating to professional and community service aspects of faculty work.

There is now a unique opportunity to enrich the preparation of those who aspire to the professoriate. One of the reasons is that a significant generational change in the faculties of the nation's colleges and universities is currently taking place. Large numbers of faculty members were hired in the 1960s and 70s as the "baby boom" generation entered college in record numbers. Those faculty and many hired since are now retiring. The United States had 1,344,000 postsecondary faculty in 2000, and will need an estimated 682,000 new faculty by 2010 to respond to an unprecedented number of retirements and to accommodate projected enrollment growth (Hecker 2001). California alone is projected to need 41,200 new full-time, tenure-track faculty between 2000 and 2010 for the University of California system, state university system, community colleges, and private institutions (Morey 2001).

The challenges facing faculty in coming years will be enormous. At a time when 75 percent of high school graduates enroll in postsecondary education within two years of graduation (The Education Trust-West 2002), students are nearly as diverse as the nation, whereas the faculties are not. Institutions of all sorts are seeking to raise the quality of education against a backdrop of public concern that college graduates lack adequate knowledge and skills that they and the country need for the future. Faculties are seeking to improve the abilities of students to think critically, solve unscripted problems, express themselves cogently both in writing and orally, and deal effectively with different peoples in a globally interdependent world. Further, the academy is largely self-regulating, and faculty participate in the shared governance of their institutions; both of these traditions are challenged by increasing requirements to be more accountable. At the very least, faculty members will need to use their expertise to creatively shape the academic profession and its institutions to meet serious educational and organizational challenges.

*PFF gives doctoral students an opportunity to experience faculty life in a protected educational context, and allows them to make an informed decision on whether they want an academic career.*

Do aspiring faculty learn about these matters in their doctoral programs and acquire capacities to meet these challenges? The answer is that too often they do not, at least not in any systematic manner. Given these changing realities, traditional doctoral preparation that focuses almost exclusively on the acquisition of scholarly or research knowledge in a field of specialization is too limited. That is why leaders of the disciplinary societies involved in this project are convinced that a larger vision of the profession is needed in their fields. Broadening the scope and raising the quality of faculty preparation— giving greater attention to

teaching, to broader definitions of scholarship, and to professional service—
are central to the future of their disciplines.

## What is PFF?

PFF is a configuration of ideas designed to promote expanded professional
development of doctoral students who are preparing for an academic career. It
embraces the doctoral degree's traditional emphasis on research, and it expands
its scope to include the broad definitions of scholarship (Boyer 1990)—discov-
ery, application, integration, and teaching. For students interested in a faculty
career, PFF introduces them to the academic profession. It also introduces
information into doctoral education about the diverse colleges and universities
that constitute the higher education landscape—with their different missions,
student bodies, and expectations for faculty. PFF gives doctoral students an
opportunity to experience faculty life in a protected educational context and
allows them to make an informed decision on whether they want an academic
career. For those who pursue an academic career, this experience helps them
prepare for a position in an institution that fits their goals and talents.
Furthermore, it provides them a competitive advantage in securing such a position and quickly establishing their new careers.

Fundamentally, PFF is based on the proposition that the doctoral experience for those interested in academic careers should a) continue to provide
opportunities to develop and obtain recognition as researchers; b) include
teaching experience that involves increasingly independent and varied responsibilities, support, and feedback; and c) offer exposure to and experience with
service to the department, campus, community, and discipline. PFF is an
intentional sequence of professional development activities.

Additional propositions that more specifically underlie various aspects of PFF include the following:

1. Apprenticeship teaching, research, and service experiences should be planned so that they are appropriate to the student's stage of professional development and progress toward the degree. For example, doctoral students assigned as teaching assistants often tend to be viewed as "covering a course section" rather than developing professional expertise benefiting themselves and students. Future faculty should be given progressively more complex assignments, more responsibility, and recognition associated with increased professional capacities.

2. Doctoral students should learn about the academic profession through exposure to the range of professional responsibilities in the variety of institutions that may become their professional homes. This exposure provides students a contextual awareness needed to find a better fit between their own interests and competencies and the needs of departments and institutions.

3. Doctoral programs should include a formalized system for mentoring in all aspects of professional development. Just as students have a mentor to guide their research, they also benefit from an ongoing relationship with an experienced faculty member as they develop their teaching and service expertise. Indeed, students can benefit from multiple mentors. A teaching mentor at a different institution, perhaps one with a mission that is distinctly different from that of the research university, may be especially valuable. The mentor program should be a primary responsibility of the director of graduate studies, the graduate committee, or the PFF director.

4. Doctoral experiences should equip future faculty for the significant changes taking place in the classrooms and curricula of today. For example, future faculty should be competent in addressing issues presented by increasing

heterogeneity among students, sophisticated about general education and inter-disciplinary curricula, and capable of using the newer, active, collaborative, technological, and experiential approaches to teaching and learning.

5. Professional development experiences should be thoughtfully integrated into the academic program and sequence of degree requirements. Unless leaders of doctoral education are intentional about these matters and structure these new experiences into their programs, PFF activities are likely to be added on to an already full program and may increase the amount of time required to earn a degree. Careful integration overcomes the tendency to add new elements without modifying existing expectations and reduces inconsistent and contradictory messages received by students. Connecting and integrating all that students do is intellectually exciting and efficient.

6. Where high-quality teaching assistant orientation and development programs are available, PFF programs should build upon them. PFF is consistent with the best practices of teaching assistant development, while also advancing another, more comprehensive level of preparation. While teaching assistant development programs can be valuable preparation for certain faculty roles, PFF programs broaden preparation by including teaching experiences at different institutions. This is particularly valuable if the student shares responsibility with an institutional faculty member or has full responsibility for planning and teaching a course. These experiences provide mentors for coaching and feedback, and engage students in various professional service and governance responsibilities.

Another key element in the PFF model is the "cluster," a new form of institutional collaboration that brings the "consumers" (institutions that employ Ph.D. faculty) together with the "producers" (the universities that educate them). A cluster is a formal, cooperative arrangement involving doctoral-

granting "anchor" universities with a range of "partner" institutions or departments in a joint working relationship. Specifically, the cluster leadership:

▲ Decides what is needed in new faculty (and it is always more than
   specialized knowledge in a discipline);
▲ Gives students opportunities to experience faculty life in multiple
   institutional settings; and
▲ Increases awareness among faculty in both the anchor and the partner
   institutions about the expectations for faculty and the ways that faculty roles are changing in various institutions.

By enriching doctoral education for the professoriate, PFF adds value to
any advanced degree program. Nonetheless, there is inertia that would maintain the status quo, and hence resist the changes PFF represents, even though
there is mounting evidence that these changes better prepare students for faculty careers.

## Overcoming Inertia

All educational innovations encounter inertia and even resistance. Educational
programs operate because some group, such as a department or an entire faculty, has deemed them important. For faculty who have arranged their professional lives around their own roles and responsibilities, any proposed change in
the way their students are prepared, even PFF, necessarily threatens the established order.

Some sources of resistance to change are particular to doctoral education,
which operates largely within a prestige economy, that is, one in which

research, grants, publications, and prizes garner prestige to faculty members and to the departments and institutions to which they belong. Graduate students are expected to help professors conduct research to further their own education, to prepare for embarking on their own career, and to accrue a scholarly reputation for their research. One common concern among both graduate faculty and graduate students is that PFF will divert students from research. Students and faculty involved in PFF programs have discovered that, while these programs do take some time, they can be designed to take relatively little. Trips to other institutions and a careful plan of activities worked out with a PFF mentor can fit into most students' schedules without undue disruption to research.

*Most graduate faculty who participate in PFF programs come to realize that each institution in the cluster has strengths and that a spirit of collaboration can draw out those strengths to benefit the career preparation and placement of students.*

The spirit of the prestige economy is competitive, not collaborative, and therefore essentially hierarchical. Research university faculty and administrators may not perceive a community college, state university, or liberal arts college to have anything of value to offer their students. However, perceptions are likely to be different in the case of universities or departments that maintain contact with their doctoral graduates who become faculty at liberal arts or community colleges or at comprehensive colleges or universities. These graduates are generally open to continuing collaborations with their research university. They can be especially effective advocates for the value of PFF activities in the doctoral education program, and they may help to form cluster collaborations. Most graduate faculty who participate in PFF programs come to realize

that each institution in the cluster has strengths and that a spirit of collaboration can draw out those strengths to benefit the career preparation and placement of students.

Funding is another concern, and some believe that dollars allocated for a
PFF program could better be used for research and direct support of talented
students. PFF leaders acknowledge that PFF programs require small amounts
of funding, though experience does not support the suggestion that PFF funds
generally derive from sources that could support research or stipends.
Increasingly, agencies that fund graduate education promote many of the
aspects of PFF as improvements in graduate programs, so establishing a PFF
program could be a positive factor in competitive funding proposals. The value
that an institution attaches to PFF determines whether it will provide funding
for the program.

Initially, partner institutions in the clusters also may be skeptical or resist-
ant. Partner faculty who serve as mentors typically are fully employed and are
concerned about finding additional time in their own schedules. In most PFF
programs, partner faculty have found that they can carve out the relatively
small amount of time required to mentor a graduate student. Partner faculty
are also concerned about compensation and recognition for their contributions. In most PFF programs, they receive modest honoraria, professional
development support, or other kinds of recognition instead of additional
salary. Further, when partner faculty are approached by a research university,
which may have been an insular neighbor, they may wonder what value they
might bring to the preparation of doctoral students, whether they are being
expected to assume the major responsibility for preparing doctoral students to
join the professoriate, and what benefits might accrue to themselves and their
institution. But after becoming acquainted with each other and working

together for some period, PFF participants typically begin to understand the strengths of the faculty at each institution, develop mutual respect, and become excited about their new roles. Moreover, most partner faculty report several intrinsic benefits from working with advanced graduate students, that are difficult to attain otherwise.

In brief, PFF leaders encounter both general and specific resistance, which most have overcome, largely by making a convincing case for the benefits of PFF to students, as well as to faculty, the department, the institution, and the discipline.

## The Need for PFF

In recent years, a good deal of empirical study has documented the need for a new approach to doctoral preparation. Studies of graduate students show a strong desire for more information about potential careers, greater attention to teaching, better mentoring, and a closer relationship between doctoral preparation and the realities of faculty work (Golde and Dore 2001; Lovitts 2001; National Association of Graduate and Professional Students 2001; Nyquist, Austin, Sprague, and Wulff 2001). For instance, from their survey in which the majority of students were in the humanities and social sciences, Golde and Dore (2001) found that, while students were satisfied overall with their doctoral experience, nearly half of the respondents recommended changes in their program. The area of greatest concern was a perceived mismatch between the training students receive and the expectations of their careers. Students especially felt unprepared for aspects of work other than research.

Studies of new faculty similarly point to the need for better graduate preparation and clearer expectations about the nature of faculty work (Rice, Sorcinelli, and Austin 2000; Sorcinelli and Trower 2001). Also supporting the

need for new approaches such as those represented by PFF is a study of doctoral recipients—some employed in the academy and some outside it—several
years after they received their degrees (Nerad and Cerney 1999). In this study
of alumni from several disciplines, respondents from all fields surveyed, but
particularly English Ph.D. graduates, were critical of their doctoral programs
for not providing adequate professional development opportunities for students and for not supporting them in their job search. Suggestions included:
enhance teacher training (the top priority among those employed in the academy), improve career and placement services, assist students to publish their
work and to attain professional visibility, broaden the educational offerings,
and increase opportunities for interdisciplinary study.

In the Nerad and Cerney study, a large fraction of respondents reported
seeking help in the job search but not obtaining enough help or the type of
help they felt they needed. For example, 41 percent of respondents who
wanted help preparing for an academic job interview reported that they never
received help, and 32 percent received "some help, but not as much as
needed." One-third sought advice on preparing a résumé, writing cover letters,
or locating job openings, but never received assistance.

A summary of these studies can be found in the summer 2002 issue of
*Liberal Education* (Gaff 2002).

## Why PFF and Disciplinary Societies?

The Pew Charitable Trusts provided the original support for PFF, which
resulted in a national competition among universities with doctoral programs
to develop model PFF programs. In the first of four related programs, the
national competition resulted in grants to graduate deans to organize univer-

## Table 1. PFF Program History

| PROJECT PHASE | DATES | GOALS | FUNDING | PARTICIPANTS |
|---|---|---|---|---|
| I | 1993-1997 | Develop model programs | The Pew Charitable Trusts | 17 anchor institutions and 68 partner institutions |
| II | 1997-2002 | Institutionalize and spread programs | The Pew Charitable Trusts | 15 anchor institutions and 119 partner institutions |
| III | 1998-2002 | Develop model programs in the sciences and mathematics | National Science Foundation | 19 departments and 92 partner departments |
| IV | 1999-2002 | Develop model programs in the humanities and social sciences | The Atlantic Philanthropies | 25 departments and 130 partner departments |

sity-wide PFF programs. These initiatives brought together clusters of diverse institutions to develop model programs based on PFF concepts (see Table 1). A subsequent grant, the second phase, allowed graduate deans to further institutionalize PFF programs, assess results, disseminate findings, and spread the PFF vision to other institutions. This strategy was successful in building a broad base of support for PFF among graduate deans, the leaders of these early initiatives, and within a limited number of disciplines, notably the humanities and social sciences.

Despite early success, the total number of graduate faculty involved in these first two phases was limited, and academic departments did not develop much sense of ownership for the PFF program. Too few faculty members were aware of the changing expectations for new faculty, the difficult job market facing their graduate students, what they could do about that market, and the potential benefits of PFF programs for their graduate students, undergraduates, and departments.

In developing the third and fourth phases of the PFF program, the PFF national leaders at CGS and AAC&U formed partnerships with disciplinary societies to harness their resources and their influence among faculty. The assumption was that, through their meetings, newsletters and other publications, and public advocacy, disciplinary societies could highlight the benefits of PFF activities to graduate as well as undergraduate students and to faculty and departments. They also can encourage graduate faculty and departments to carefully compare the expectations of new faculty with the preparation students receive in their graduate programs and to align doctoral programs more closely with expectations.

Doctoral education is a powerful socialization experience in which academic departments play primary roles. It is through doctoral education that scholars in a field of specialization educate future practitioners and cultivate their capacities to make advances in the field. Leaders of the disciplinary societies that have embraced PFF have discovered that PFF creates synergy with other national agendas of the societies, such as efforts to diversify the faculty, improve the teaching of new faculty, encourage social and community engagement, and explore the scholarship of teaching and learning.

The third phase of PFF was funded by the National Science Foundation (NSF) and involved partnerships in the biological and life sciences, chemistry, computer science, mathematics, and physics (Pruitt-Logan, Gaff, and Jentoft 2002). Societies in each discipline conducted a national competition among departments and awarded grants to develop model PFF programs. Originally, a society in the biological and life sciences agreed to participate but withdrew because it reported little interest in PFF among its members. The PFF office subsequently served as a surrogate for the biology association in soliciting pro-posals and found significant interest among universities. Each selected depart-ment created a cluster of departments in different kinds of institutions to collec-tively design and implement the PFF program. The societies provided technical assistance to the clusters, highlighted their work at meetings and in publications, and interpreted the innovations in faculty preparation to their memberships.

A fourth phase of PFF, which is the focus of this volume, involved collabo-ration with the disciplinary societies in the social sciences and humanities listed below.

- ▲ American Historical Association
- ▲ American Political Science Association
- ▲ American Psychological Association
- ▲ American Sociological Association
- ▲ National Communication Association
- ▲ National Council of Teachers of English

Support for the fourth phase of PFF was provided by The Atlantic Philanthropies, which, like the other two funding agencies, was primarily inter-ested in improving undergraduate education. The support of innovations in graduate education was intended as a means to enhance the learning of under-graduates.

## What Did the Disciplinary Societies Do?

The structure of the fourth phase is similar to that of the third. Each of the societies conducted a national competition in the spring of 2000 that resulted in matching grants to academic departments to create model PFF programs. In addition, they provided technical assistance to those departments, assisted with the assessment of programs, highlighted PFF programs at their regular meetings and in their publications, and generally promoted PFF as a beneficial way to educate future faculty in their fields. More details about the activities of the societies are provided in chapter four. The national PFF office coordinated work among the disciplinary societies and also conducted summer working conferences, operated a national PFF network, disseminated information, and served as a national advocate for PFF initiatives.

Twenty-five academic departments were selected to participate in this project: five in English and four each in communication, history, political science, psychology, and sociology. The departments, the name of a contact person, and the partner institutions in each cluster are listed in Appendix II. Each department organized a cluster of departments in its discipline, and each cluster, by design, represents the variety of higher education institutions likely to hire new faculty. Fourteen departments were located on campuses with existing university-wide PFF programs, nine were stand-alone programs on campuses without either a centralized program or a program in other departments, and two were on the same campus. Although social science and humanities faculty and doctoral students had been involved in the earlier PFF phase one and phase two projects, this volume is based largely on the experiences of the disciplinary societies and the departmental clusters with which they worked during phase four.

During the first two PFF phases, graduate deans provided leadership to engage graduate faculty and to secure a sense of ownership for departmentally based PFF programs. They identified certain academic departments as loci for creating PFF programs, recruited key faculty to participate, and obtained departmental approval for students to participate. In phases three and four, departments were invited to identify a faculty principal investigator and to apply to their respective disciplinary society for a grant to implement a PFF program. During the process of applying for a grant, principal investigators sought the involvement of departmental colleagues and the support of graduate and academic deans. The grant proposal required letters of support from the graduate dean, dean of the arts and sciences unit, and chief academic officer at the university and from the department chair and academic dean at the partner institutions. In addition, the university was required to match grant funds, often with resources from the graduate or academic deans, or from the department. If a centralized PFF program had been established on the campus, departments were urged to take advantage of these resources as well, in the belief that doctoral education works best when the department, the university, and other institutional partners work together to support a broader education for doctoral students.

The disciplinary societies used the following criteria to select departments:

▲ Commitment to PFF concepts
▲ Commitment to create and lead a cluster that included departments in partner institutions
▲ Evidence of enrolling and graduating traditionally underrepresented graduate student populations and plans to continue to do so
▲ Likelihood of sustainability after the funding period
▲ Willingness and ability to disseminate information about PFF: to other departments within the discipline, throughout the university, and at national meetings
▲ Feasibility of the program design
▲ Willingness to participate in assessment activities
▲ Commitment of institutional funds to match their awards

Table 2 lists the numbers and types of colleges and universities in the fourth PFF phase.

## Table 2. Distribution of Institutions Participating in Phase Four PFF by Discipline

| Type of Institution | History | Political Science | Psychology | Sociology | Communication | English | TOTAL |
|---|---|---|---|---|---|---|---|
| Doctoral | 5 | 8* | 7 | 7 | 8 | 7 | 42 |
| Masters | 10 | 8 | 5 | 14 | 10 | 5 | 52 |
| Baccalaureate | 1 | 5 | 6 | 3 | 6 | 1 | 22 |
| Associate | 6 | 6 | 3 | 3 | 7 | 9 | 34 |
| Specialized | 1 | 1 | 1 | 0 | 2 | 0 | 5 |
| TOTAL | 23 | 28 | 22 | 27 | 33 | 22 | 155 |

*Includes Stanford University, which collaborated with the University of Colorado in a joint PFF project.*

Across all disciplines, 70 percent of the institutions were non-doctoral granting, which approximates the 64 percent of the faculty in higher education who are employed at non-doctoral institutions (American Council on Education 2001). The institutions included 42 doctoral, 52 master's, 22 baccalaureate, 34 associate, and 5 specialized. The clusters reflect the rich diversity of American higher education and expose graduate students to quite different institutional missions, histories, campus cultures, and student bodies—and hence, different expectations for faculty.

## How Do PFF Programs Operate?

Campus leaders are encouraged to develop PFF programs that are both in keeping with PFF concepts and reflect their particular needs, interests, and circumstances. PFF programs concentrate activities in three loci: the *department*, because some learning is particular to the disciplines; the *university*, because some learning is general and appropriate for all PFF students; and the *partner institutions*, because some learning is dependent on the institutional context.

*Departments* typically provide sequences of supervised teaching experiences, offer a course on the teaching of their discipline, coordinate their activities with the center for teaching and learning and other resources, host discussions in which faculty members from different institutions describe their careers, and sponsor talks by alumni in which they discuss their experience as new faculty and the adequacy of their preparation.

*University* activities typically include forums on faculty life and careers, discussions of faculty governance issues, a course on the general topic of college teaching and learning, and development of professional portfolios documenting student expertise in teaching, research, and service.

*Partner institutions* often assign a mentor to work with doctoral students, invite students to attend department or faculty meetings, include them in faculty development activities, and offer supervised teaching opportunities.

The specific kinds of program elements developed by the social science and humanities departments in this project are discussed in Chapter 3.

## What Insights Have Been Gained From the PFF Initiative?

Numerous assessments have been conducted since PFF programs began. The major lessons learned from these assessments are:

▲  It is possible for institutions as dissimilar as doctoral degree granting and primarily undergraduate institutions to collaborate in the preparation of aspiring faculty;

▲ Regardless of the variety in content and implementation among programs, PFF programs broaden the background of participating students in ways that better prepare them for the many roles expected of
new faculty;

▲ Doctoral students and alumni are enthusiastic about the benefits of
their PFF programs, which include learning about the academic profession and developing a competitive advantage on the job market;

▲ Faculty members from partner institutions enjoy working with doctoral students and derive benefits that apply to their own professional
development;

▲ Graduate faculty members appreciate the professional development
their students receive through PFF programs;

▲ Virtually everyone involved in PFF would recommend the program to
others; and

▲ Benefits to academic departments and universities include better
recruitment, greater satisfaction among graduate students, and better
placement. These benefits outweigh the modest investments of time
and money that are required.

Recognizing that more assessment is needed, especially related to the long-
term and possible unintended consequences of PFF programs, The Atlantic
Philanthropies and NSF have jointly commissioned a three-year independent
assessment of the PFF initiative through all four phases, and these data are
gradually becoming available. The early results generally confirm the positive
findings of the assessments of PFF; they are discussed further in chapter five.

# Chapter 2

# Strategies for Establishing a PFF Program

*The PFF experience has allowed me to gain experience in
teaching at an institution other than a research institution so
that I can make some decisions about the type of institution—
teaching or research—where I would eventually like to work.*
—Graduate Student in English, University of Illinois, Chicago

After two years of participation in the phase four humanities and social science
PFF program, faculty were asked to reflect on their experiences and to share
with their colleagues across the range of doctoral programs in their disciplines
what they had learned about starting PFF programs. In this chapter, participants' responses are summarized, quoted, or paraphrased as a means of convey-
ing recommended actions and activities for graduate and partner faculty to
consider or undertake when they create a PFF program.

## Secure Leadership

The humanities and social science PFF programs in this project were largely
initiated by department faculty, some acting in their capacity as department
chair or director of graduate studies. Graduate deans and directors of teaching-
learning centers also contributed to program development. Experience
throughout the four phases of PFF confirms that a PFF program can be initiated by anyone who has standing in graduate education, is aware of the advantages offered by a PFF program, and is willing to work with various con-

stituencies to forge a supportive coalition for broadening the graduate education of students who may become faculty members in the discipline.

Before the program begins, a faculty member who shares the ideals of PFF must be identified to serve as the director. The director must recognize that graduate education is a collective responsibility of the faculty and develop a departmental consensus for launching a PFF program. Moreover, it is essential that graduate faculty be supportive and that they encourage their students to participate in PFF, for it is faculty commitment that will sustain the program. Several PFF leaders have also found it a good strategy to connect a new PFF program to a previously sanctioned departmental activity.

Barbara Risman, Director of Graduate Studies in sociology at North Carolina State University, says,

*"It really makes it easy if the PFF organizer is also the Director of Graduate Studies, and the graduate committee sees this as part of their purview. It avoids being an 'add on' to already burdened faculty."*

## Identify Cluster Partners

The core of a PFF program is the cluster, a configuration of institutions representing the diversity of American colleges and universities, anchored by a Ph.D. degree-granting department. The task of creating a cluster of different kinds of institutions—the most distinguishing element in PFF programs—is often complex. The cluster of diverse institutions, such as liberal arts colleges, comprehensive universities, and community colleges, represents the variety of institutional contexts where graduate students might pursue a career. In some cases, institutions or departments may have already established connections that are easily transformed into a PFF partnership. In many instances, however, PFF

partnerships may represent a new form of collaboration that may require institutions to overcome a history of competition or of stereotyping, and to foster a
spirit of cooperation to better prepare the next generation of faculty members.

Those organizing PFF programs must confront issues of prestige, perceptions of colleagues at different institutions, and the value that faculty from different institutions bring to the graduate experience of doctoral students. For
instance, at certain institutions, faculty might think of themselves as more
accomplished researchers, more effective teachers, or more committed to educating a diverse student body than the faculty at other institutions. But when faculty members become acquainted and begin to collaborate, they soon understand that such views are simplistic and that the common hierarchies by which
institutions are ranked are counterproductive. They realize that there are
strengths among faculty at each type of institution and that these can be of
advantage to a PFF program.

Issues that arise in organizing clusters include administrative complexity
and the corresponding time required to recruit, organize, and maintain the
clusters. When a university has an established, centralized PFF program (as in
the case of institutions that participated in the first two PFF phases), the task
of organizing a departmental cluster may be relatively easy. The PFF director
can take advantage of existing cluster arrangements developed by the graduate
school. For example, both Howard University and the University of Nebraska
established PFF clusters in the phases preceding this PFF project. Therefore,
when the department of communication at these universities wished to create
PFF programs, they were able to build on the continuing relationships with
partner institutions. On the other hand, the departments of sociology at North
Carolina State University and Texas A&M University were the first to initiate
PFF programs at their institutions. Consequently, the departmental PFF
organizers had to contact colleagues in sociology departments at other institu-

tions and invite them to participate as "partner institutions" in a grant application and in the subsequent PFF program. "For stand-alone PFF programs like ours," writes Robin Fleming, director of the history PFF program at Boston College, "it is important to keep the program simple. We have had much better luck organizing programs and events that include the participation of one local school, rather than two or three." As the program grows and positive experiences increase, more institutions can be added.

One of the challenges of the cluster concept is to explain what PFF and the anchor institution can offer partner faculty, departments, and institutions. This should be carefully considered before any contact is made, since partner school representatives often raise this issue early in discussions about establishing a cluster.

A number of relationships may already exist between research universities and potential partner institutions, including research and educational collaborations between faculty members and administrators. Partner faculty may also be graduates of the department establishing the PFF program, and they often welcome an opportunity to "give back" something of value to their graduate program. Thus, they are often effective advocates for the PFF program and can be asked to facilitate interactions between the two faculties. These pre-existing ties can be the starting points for developing clusters. Once potential partner faculty members are identified, an initial meeting where the goals of PFF are explained and program possibilities are presented has proved to be a good recruiting strategy. Once partner faculty are involved in the program, they can be asked to recruit additional colleagues.

One of the initial steps is for the collaborating faculty members at the graduate and partner institutions to become acquainted and to establish mutual trust, according to Noel Stowe, director of the history PFF program at Arizona State University (ASU). Two PFF summer conferences brought the

ASU cluster members together for several days, and Stowe credits those experiences with developing a rapport among fellow historians as they learned about each other and discussed common interests.

## Appoint a Steering Committee

All relevant constituencies from participating institutions should be involved in the process of defining PFF program goals, planning program activities, and developing long-range plans. For this reason, PFF leaders in the social sciences and humanities recommend forming a steering committee that (1) includes doctoral students, (2) is manageable in size, (3) meets on different campuses, and (4) is representative of faculty at both the partner institutions and the graduate university. In fact, to ensure that the partners have a strong voice, the steering committee of the ASU department of history PPF program is structured to require the number of partner institution members to equal or exceed the number of ASU members. The role of the steering committee is to assess members' perspectives on the preparation of future faculty, understand differences in the academic cultures of partner institutions, and recognize the potential contributions that each institution in the cluster can make to the program.

Once a PFF program has begun, leaders have found it valuable for the steering committee to shift its focus from program planning to oversight. They suggest that the committee meet at least once per academic term to inform participants about program activities and to discuss program-related issues. Continuing opportunities to communicate across constituencies and reaffirm involvement are critical elements to an effective PFF program. In order to facilitate communication, each partner institution usually designates one contact person who is familiar with and actively participates in and supports the program. Many programs appoint a senior graduate student as PFF administrative assistant. This provides a valuable experience for the student, since the assistant is at the hub of program planning and administration and sees the program from the perspectives of all constituencies. Because communication among all participants is vital, some programs have developed a PFF cluster Web site or an electronic listserve.

## Recruit Doctoral Student Participants

Graduate students are eager to participate in professional development activities, and recruiting them is among the easiest tasks in launching a PFF program. Indeed, doctoral students are perhaps the best advocates and the best recruiters for PFF, often through informal conversations with their peers. Just as in other areas, word of mouth seems to be among the most effective means of advertising PFF.

**Attracting students.** Doctoral students are attracted to PFF for a variety of reasons. Some are certain they want an academic career and seek to learn as much as they can about their chosen profession. Others want to explore the possibility of a faculty career and wish to learn about faculty roles at a variety of institutions. Many say they would like to enhance their teaching abilities and acquire credentials. Nearly all want to be more competitive in securing their first academic position and believe that PFF participation gives them a competitive advantage.

Although most PFF programs target students who have chosen an academic career goal, those who are ambivalent about an academic career constitute another pool of potential recruits. Rosemary Phelps, who leads the psychology PFF program at the University of Georgia, advocates identifying students with the potential for a successful academic career and exploring this alternative with them. One way to appeal to students who are ambivalent about an academic career is to arrange open forums for students on such topics as what students expect from their doctoral degree work, what the expectations of faculty are at various types of institutions, and what the department can do to facilitate progress toward a degree. John Reilly, who directs the PFF program in English at Howard University writes, "When they [students] realize that the life of a professor really is about more than making life hard for apprentices, they are ready to be introduced to a PFF program. Once they become PFF participants, they enjoy other opportunities, such as co-authorship of papers, paid membership in disciplinary societies, and travel to deliver presentations at disciplinary conferences."

**Students of color.** From the beginning of this project, PFF clusters in the social sciences and humanities have been committed to addressing the underrepresentation of persons of color among college and university faculty in their disciplines by ensuring that students of color participate in PFF programs. PFF leaders have succeeded in increasing participation of students of color by connecting their recruitment efforts to those of institutional programs that address similar concerns. The sociology PFF program at the University of Nebraska, Lincoln, exemplifies this approach. The PFF program's recruiting efforts build upon the institution's Ronald E. McNair Postbaccalaureate Achievement Program, sponsored by the U.S. Department of Education. The McNair program prepares underrepresented undergraduate students for graduate studies through involvement in research and other scholarly activities.

Howard University programs in communication, history, and political science offer another example of attracting students of color, in this case through linking to the university's Graduate Assistance in Areas of National Need (GAANN) program. The U.S. Department of Education's GAANN program requires grantees to establish policies and procedures to ensure that talented students from traditionally underrepresented backgrounds are actively recruited to the GAANN program; hence these programs are natural partners for PFF.

Robert Robinson, Chair of the Department of Sociology at Indiana University, writes that a departmental poster designed to recruit students highlights the PFF program and its commitment to training outstanding scholars and teachers. The poster was sent to universities with high minority enrollments, including historically black colleges and universities, Hispanic-serving institutions, and tribal colleges.

Many students, especially students of color, emphasize that service is important in their lives and that they want public service to be an integral part of their professional career. PFF can help all students recognize that service is a broad concept that involves more than direct work with clients or the traditional committee work of faculty. According to Julio Rojas, a PFF student in psychology at the University of Georgia, some students of color realize that, as future members of the academy, they can provide leadership for service learning and thereby maintain their core values (Rojas 2002).

A commitment to developing a broad understanding by all students of the issue of student diversity and how it relates to faculty work can serve as an effective recruiting tool. Many of the phase four PFF programs intentionally included institutions that have a more diverse student body than that of the graduate university. Thus, the English PFF programs at Michigan Tech University and Washington State University both include tribal colleges in their clusters, and both report that students in these programs gained a much broader and more useful understanding of diversity through their experiences on these cluster campuses.

**Program flexibility.** PFF leaders report that flexibility in the PFF program allows doctoral students to participate when and for as long as they are interested. Some first and second year doctoral students find that PFF programs complement teaching assistant training and enhance their contribution to the department's undergraduate teaching efforts. Those students further along in their graduate program may benefit more from participating in intensive teaching activities at cluster institutions, such as co-teaching a course or a portion of a course with a mentor at the cluster institution, or being responsible for an entire course. Students in the later stages of their doctoral work also benefit from participating in service activities, such as faculty governance and public outreach. Many PFF programs pay special attention to developing effective writing and communications skills. Some programs also include grant-writing activities, since some new assistant professors will be expected to generate external support for their research.

**Student recognition.** Typically, PFF programs offer participants graduate credit for courses. Some give a certificate for participation, and others note PFF participation on the transcript. Regardless of how it is conferred, recognition of student participation is an important element of a PFF program. The presence on the résumé and transcript of a formally documented PFF experience may significantly improve a doctoral student's chance of obtaining an academic position at an institution at which good teaching and service are especially important criteria for new faculty hires. Such documentation also helps to create a market demand for the type of faculty preparation that PFF provides, by informing faculty search committees about special qualities of these candidates.

## Design Mentoring Activities

Mentoring of graduate students by both graduate and partner faculty is a key component of a PFF program. Although the relationship between doctoral student and dissertation research mentor is usually well defined, the PFF mentoring relationship typically is more flexible and is designed to meet the particular professional development needs of the doctoral student. A unique advantage of the PFF program is that participating students have access to at least one mentor besides their research adviser. This allows students to establish relationships with faculty members with expertise in teaching and service as well as in their content specialties.

One of the most powerful innovations of PFF is the unique opportunity for doctoral students to work with a faculty mentor at a partner institution. This arrangement allows doctoral students to establish a relationship with a faculty member who can introduce them to specific challenges of teaching that institution's student body, the expectations and support for faculty research, and the roles of faculty members in the shared governance of that department or institution. "They learn what you do with your time," says Kathrynn Adams, a Guilford College psychology professor who mentors Duke University students. "They learn about academic life, rather than psychology *per se*" (quoted in Murray 2000 p. 65).

The process of matching PFF mentors to students varies. Some directors collect résumés from faculty and allow doctoral students to choose mentors, or vice versa. Often the assignment results from a process of exchanging information between faculty and students until a preferred choice emerges. Sometimes doctoral students visit a partner institution and meet with potential mentors. If a suitable relationship with one of these faculty members is agreed to, the mentoring relationship commences.

Regardless of how the relationship is established, it is important for both parties to decide on specific goals, activities, means of assessment and feedback, and the amount of time required. In the sociology PFF program at the University of Nebraska, Lincoln (UNL), both student and mentor sign an agreement in which the student agrees to participate in activities such as attending a colloquium on conducting classroom research, working with the mentor to explore a service opportunity, and discussing the co-authorship of a potential publication. The mentor agrees to undertake responsibilities such as conferring with the student on his/her proposed capstone project, collaborating on identifying appropriate teaching opportunities, and discussing whether co-authorship of a publication is appropriate and of mutual benefit (see Appendix III for the UNL mentoring contract).

PFF leaders emphasize that an effective mentoring relationship requires mutual respect and that the mentoring process is reciprocal; that is, the relationship requires input and effort from, and usually has positive outcomes for, both graduate students and faculty.

## Secure the Support of Graduate and Partner Faculty

Graduate faculty members participate in a PFF program in a variety of ways. They serve as mentors to help doctoral students develop their skills in teaching, research, and professional service; and they advise students on classroom practices, pedagogy, presentations, and other aspects of an academic profession. They also participate in PFF seminars and workshops, and they offer suggestions for improving the program. They often facilitate interactions between doctoral students and partner institution faculty. Most also discuss faculty roles with their students and encourage those who might be interested in academic careers to participate in the PFF program.

One important role for departmental faculty who may not be directly involved in the program is to voice support for PFF and to encourage appropriate students to participate. Some doctoral students report receiving mixed messages from the graduate faculty and other doctoral students: some faculty members encourage participation in PFF, while others discourage any activity that takes time away from research. Given the department faculty's collective responsibility for their department's graduate program, once a department decides to offer a PFF program, faculty members who do not wish to participate should (at the very least) not discourage students from taking part.

It is essential that graduate faculty recognize the PFF program as an integral part of the department's graduate program. Victor Benassi, director of the psychology PFF program at the University of New Hampshire, writes that in reports to his colleagues, he includes information about the national initiative as well. He focuses on ways that faculty can participate and on the advantage their participation has for their students. He observes that when graduate faculty take part in PFF, they learn of their colleagues' perceptions of the initiative as well as how students are responding to the program. PFF leaders in social sciences and humanities report that most graduate faculty members have been generous with their time and expertise when asked by the program director to take a doctoral student to a committee meeting, for example, or to a national disciplinary conference. Once involved, faculty members tend to be supportive of students' participation in PFF. In general, less involved graduate faculty in the humanities and social sciences present little active resistance to the participation of their students in PFF activities.

Service on a standing PFF committee is considered a regular departmental assignment for history department faculty at Florida State University, according to PFF director Jonathan Grant. Because faculty members receive service credit for PFF committee work, PFF work is not an "add on," but rather an integrated part of departmental service. As faculty awareness of and receptivity to PFF goals develop within the department, interest in serving on the PFF committees increases.

Like graduate faculty, partner faculty members play essential and distinctive roles in PFF programs. Although their involvement varies among programs, typical activities include designing and implementing doctoral student internships, participating in workshops, giving conference presentations on PFF, lecturing in graduate PFF courses, sharing their experiences as faculty at very different types of institutions, and supervising students' teaching responsibilities at their institutions. According to Barbara Risman, director of the PFF program in sociology at North Carolina State University, involvement of partner faculty is highly successful. Partner faculty members participate on panel discussions open to all graduate students, covering such topics as the realities of their jobs and the way hiring decisions are made at their institutions. These sorts of activities require partner institution faculty members to be involved in academic programs at research universities.

Partner faculty and graduate faculty both feel obligated to provide opportunities for doctoral students to participate in PFF. They also view the opportunity to interact and work with PFF participants as a major benefit to faculty. Moreover, partner faculty themselves benefit from a closer relationship with the academic department at the research university, a relationship that sometimes leads to collaboration on other professional projects. Some partner schools that employ adjunct faculty regard PFF programs as reliable sources of motivated and effective instructors. These schools sometimes recruit PFF students as adjunct faculty to serve as sabbatical replacements or to offer courses in subjects not currently available at the partner institution. In some instances, the student is later recruited by the institution or recommended to other institutions for a permanent faculty position. PFF students also give talks to enrich the partner institution's program, and they can provide links to faculty members at the research university who are willing to assist with research projects that involve undergraduate students, thus providing new opportunities for the partner schools' undergraduates.

## Obtain Funding

Those involved in the leadership of a PFF program, whether departmental or university-wide, know that establishing and maintaining a program requires some money, though generally not large amounts. Typically, funds are used for a variety of programmatic activities, such as student and faculty travel to partner institutions, student travel to professional meetings, printing of newsletters in which students report on their PFF experiences and what they learned, and meals and snacks for PFF meetings. Securing budgetary support is one of the key indicators that a program can be sustained after it is launched with a grant.

The grants to departments in this fourth phase of PFF were small: $10,000 for each of two years, matched by institutional funds. Departments were allowed to use grant funds for a variety of programmatic activities, such as those mentioned above.

The matching funds came from various sources—the academic department, graduate school, academic dean's office, and teaching and learning center. Institutional funds were used to provide student stipends, to supplement faculty salaries, or to provide honoraria for partner faculty. To supplement grant funds, PFF directors and graduate deans have also been particularly creative in linking PFF program concepts to proposals for funding from related graduate education initiatives. For example, the GAANN Program at Howard University requires GAANN participants to participate in the university's PFF program, thus providing supplemental stipend support for PFF participants.

Most PFF cluster leaders anticipate a continuation of PFF after the grant period, although for a few public institutions in states projecting reduced revenues and smaller higher education budgets, there are concerns that such constraints might make it difficult for universities to support even a successful PFF program. Since budgets, however, always reflect values and priorities, such contingencies could be countered by building a coalition of support for PFF in the form of a critical mass of students and faculty members who know from experience the benefits that PFF provides.

Having considered the elements needed to start PFF programs, we turn in the next chapter to the array of activities that constitute the substance of PFF programs.

# Chapter 3

# Content of PFF Programs

> *Systematic attention to program flexibility and*
> *individualized student attention can have positive results.*
> *We have found that a "cookie-cutter" approach to a PFF*
> *program does not always address PFF student concerns or needs.*
>
> —Graduate Student in Psychology, University of Georgia

Common PFF program elements include courses for credit, certificate programs, seminars, workshops and informal student activities, experiences at
partner institutions, professional activities, and attention to diversity. While
PFF programs do not necessarily include all these elements, examples are presented below that illustrate the various ways these elements have been used and
assembled in PFF programs.

## Courses for Credit

Courses are the primary means by which education programs are organized,
and this is true for PFF, as the following examples illustrate.

The program in English at the University of South Florida offers a course
entitled "Professional Identities in Rhetoric and Composition." The course fea-
tures guest speakers who address various professional opportunities, such as
positions teaching at vocational and community colleges and teaching English
as a Second Language, as well as positions in writing center administration,
writing programs, and adult literacy programs.

At the University of Illinois at Chicago, Dick Simpson created two new sequential PFF courses that are the building blocks of the PFF program in political science: "Introduction to the Political Science Profession" and "Teaching Political Science." The first course is required of all new Ph.D. students, and the second is required for teaching assistants and strongly encouraged for those interested in an academic career.

*The goal of PFF is to integrate courses and activities into the academic program and sequence of degree requirements.*

Howard University PFF students in communication take an on-line teaching course using pre-packaged software to expand their understanding of technology in the classroom. The course also enhances their ability to conduct a technology-augmented class. Arizona State University's PFF program in history, in collaboration with the College of Extended Education, developed a one-semester associateship for teaching and managing an online introductory freshman course for the department.

The department of history at Florida State University offers a course entitled "Teaching in the Discipline," in which students practice the skills they will use in the classroom. This course is taught by a graduate faculty member and includes presentations by partner faculty about their teaching goals and experiences at their own institutions. This course has become an effective venue for raising awareness of the challenges of being a faculty member at different types of institutions.

The goal of PFF is to integrate courses and activities into the academic program and sequence of degree requirements. Recognizing that students need to know what to expect so that they can be prepared for the opportunities that may become available during their graduate program, Arizona State University (ASU) includes PFF information in the orientation program for new doctoral students. PFF courses are not intended simply as additions to already crowded doctoral requirements. According to Noel Stowe, director of ASU's history PFF program, PFF courses and activities can be offered over an extended period of a student's program, rather than telescoped into a particular semester or year of doctoral work.

The experience of a student in the University of Illinois at Chicago English PFF program illustrates how PFF can further research interests. The student's dissertation dealing with the conditions of faculty at local community colleges evolved from a PFF course entitled "Pedagogy and the Profession." The thesis is credited with helping the student secure a tenure-track position at Elmhurst College.

## Certificate Programs

Many PFF programs in social sciences and humanities have developed certificate programs as a means of recognizing student achievements. Certificate programs provide the opportunity to earn a formal credential that is part of the student's permanent academic record.

Indiana University's department of communication and culture offers a Certificate of Pedagogy. The culminating pedagogy course, according to PFF director Patricia Andrews, addresses such pragmatic concerns as finishing the dissertation, publishing, creating a teaching portfolio, entering the academic job market, preparing for an interview, preparing a job talk, and navigating the road to tenure. The course also includes controversial issues, such as challenges to liberal learning in the 21$^{st}$ century, assessment, communication across the curriculum, service learning and civic engagement, distance education, and diversity in higher education. To earn the certificate, students are required to complete three courses and pass a one-hour doctoral qualifying examination focused on pedagogy. Students also create teaching portfolios, prepare a résumé, participate in a mock job interview, design a course that blends their teaching and research interests, and give a job talk.

The department of sociology at Indiana University also offers a distinct certificate program. A teaching certificate is awarded upon completion of the following three-course sequence: "The Teaching of Undergraduate Sociology," "Sociological Issues in College Pedagogy," and "Research Seminar on the Scholarship of Teaching and Learning."

Through the Council for Excellence in Teaching and Learning (CETL) at the University of Illinois, Chicago, PFF director Dick Simpson offers a series of workshops on teaching techniques in conjunction with the course, "Teaching Political Science." CETL provides students with a certificate in teaching for those who take the PFF course, attend three CETL workshops, and create their own teaching portfolios.

## Seminars, Workshops, and Informal Student Activities

Less formal seminars, workshops, and student activities also offer exposure to career issues and teaching and learning concepts. Typically, the graduate school is the sponsor of PFF seminars and workshops. At these events, former PFF students discuss their PFF experiences and how best to prepare for a faculty position at their type of institution. Informal brown bag luncheons are another venue for providing doctoral students with information about faculty careers. In other cases, graduate schools invite students to attend seminars led by nationally recognized leaders in the graduate community.

In the department of sociology at the University of Nebraska, Lincoln, students participate in a workshop on classroom research and evaluation strategies that draws from the work of Cross and Steadman (1996) and Angelo and Cross (1993). According to PFF director Helen Moore, students create a project on the scholarship of teaching and learning. Students then prepare a proposal, complete with a statement of pedagogical goals, lesson plans, and institutional review board approvals for evaluation strategies, after examining a range of classroom evaluation techniques.

Melbourne Cummings, director of the PFF program in communication at Howard University, reports that the program requires students to attend workshops that address a variety of issues such as diversity in the classroom and at the university, classroom management, grant writing and its importance for conducting research, university and departmental politics, faculty governance, and departmental leadership. Faculty and administrators from the department of communication and culture—as well as from other university departments—lead these discussions. The list of speakers has included a member of the board of trustees, the president, and the provost.

Jeanne Toungara, Howard University's PFF director in history, also conducts an extensive group of PFF student workshops. Sample titles include "The Teaching Portfolio," "The Institutional Review Board," and "The First Year of Teaching."

It is well known that student learning is not limited to formal courses, seminars, and other formal credit-bearing activities. Informal activities play a role as well. Victor Benassi, director of the University of New Hampshire's PFF psychology program, reports that students in his program participate in a uni-

versity-wide PFF breakfast series, an informal activity at which issues related to
faculty careers are discussed with partner faculty. According to Robin Fleming,
director of the history PFF program at Boston College, graduate students in
the department eagerly sign up for PFF activities that have some practical
application, such as those that deal with technology, hands-on-teaching, or
job-market preparation. Leaders in the graduate student government organization like to be involved in planning PFF events and willingly participate in
programs that they help organize.

## Experiences at Partner Institutions

The landscape of doctoral education is dotted with partnerships between colleges and doctoral universities to strengthen the education of aspiring faculty.
Although PFF is a strong proponent of partnering, it can still be a challenge to
identify partners and create ways to collaborate. It is important to be flexible in
the ways PFF students become involved on partner campuses so that their
involvement includes a broad range of faculty responsibilities.

Cecilia Shore, PFF director at Miami University of Ohio explains that
PFF students in the department of psychology have served as reviewers of
undergraduate research submissions to a regional conference, provided statisti-
cal consulting for a survey of student satisfaction on a partner campus, and
shadowed partner faculty as they attended campus governance meetings.

When PFF began in 1994, guidelines stated that partner institutions
should be within easy commuting distance of the anchor university. The
activities cited below, however, show that partnerships need not be limited by
distance.

According to Patricia Andrews, PFF director at Indiana University's department of communication and culture, when students in that program traveled to

Arizona State University-West, they shadowed faculty, offered colloquia, talked with students, dined with the dean, and attended a faculty meeting. Similar activities were involved in a trip to a different type of partner institution, Texas A&M-Kingsville. They learned that Indiana University differs from both partner institutions in student diversity and faculty roles.

Teaching internships at partner institutions are common elements of PFF programs. Noel Stowe writes that the history PFF program he directs at ASU has developed an internship program with one of the ASU branch campuses, so that a student nearing completion of the doctorate can have an independent teaching opportunity with undergraduate students whose interests and degree programs differ from those that characterize the main campus. The English PFF program at the University of South Florida has created fellowships so its students can teach as interns at a partner institution. In the PFF program in sociology at Indiana University, students serve in semester-long placements at other campuses in the state system and, with extensive supervision, teach their own courses that match the needs of the partner institution and undergraduate students.

*Teaching internships at partner institutions are common elements of PFF programs.*

## Professional Activities

Experiences of PFF students are enriched through participation in professional activities in regional and national settings. Each of the participating humanities and social science disciplinary societies has featured graduate students at major conferences. In joint presentations with their mentors, students acquaint audiences with the advantages of having PFF programs on university campuses and talk about their own research and how their scholarly interests influenced their pedagogy. There are also international venues for professional development. PFF students in the communication department at Howard University gave papers at international conferences in Hong Kong, West Indies, Japan, and Canada.

In addition to attending conferences devoted to their disciplines, one PFF student from each cluster in every discipline was invited to attend the 2002 annual meeting of the Association of American Colleges and Universities. The twelve students who participated said attendance enhanced their understanding of such issues as changing faculty roles, hiring practices, and support for new faculty. They also were able to network with peer PFF students from different schools and disciplines, observe their future colleagues addressing national issues in higher education, and interact with academic officers at different kinds of institutions. The American Political Science Association reports that in a survey of political science PFF students, peer networks were important to a greater percentage of respondents than was faculty assistance.

## Attention to Diversity

Diversity is a critically important element of any PFF program. Diversity issues are incorporated in several ways in humanities and social sciences PFF programs. Examples include learning to teach for inclusiveness and experiencing racially and ethnically diverse institutions.

The campus-wide ASU PFF program—which includes students in the social sciences and humanities—incorporates activities that focus on teaching for inclusiveness. Promoting inclusiveness draws attention to a range of nontraditional students such as persons with disabilities and parents who are work-ing while attending college, as well as racial and ethnic minorities. Because diversity is the overarching concept that ties the program's modules together, all panelists in the ASU seminar series—from within and outside the university—are asked to address the topic. Such consistent and repeated emphasis is a good strategy for producing understanding of diversity issues. One seminar is devoted exclusively to teaching and learning in the inclusive classroom. It includes the following topics: being a member of an underrepresented group in the discipline, speaking from a position of privilege in the class-room, addressing sensitive topics, connecting with students with disabilities, and the burden of trying to represent all members of an ethnic group.

*Because diversity is the overarching concept that ties the program's modules together, all seminar panelists— from within and outside the university— are asked to address the topic.*

Several clusters include institutions with large numbers of racial and ethnic minority stu-dents, and their presence helps PFF students understand a variety of institutional missions, curricular issues, and approaches to teaching and learning. Little Priest Tribal College, which enrolls American Indian students, partners with the PFF sociol-ogy program at the University of Nebraska, Lincoln. The Michigan Technological University and Washington State University English programs both cluster with tribal colleges. Communication, political science, and history PFF students at Howard University, most of whom are from underrepresented racial or ethnic groups, have opportunities to experience predominantly white universities. The Catholic University of America and Marymount University

were early members of the Howard cluster, and other institutions with predominantly white enrollments later joined the cluster. They include Virginia
Polytechnic Institute and State University, the University of New Hampshire,
and Hope College.

A disciplinary society can provide leadership in addressing the discipline's
underrepresentation of students of color. One example is the American
Sociological Association's Minority Opportunities through School
Transformation (MOST) program. MOST is designed to achieve excellence
and inclusiveness in colleges and universities by fostering intentional and systemic change at the department level. Operating in eleven institutions, MOST
has increased the number of courses dealing with diversity, the number of
graduating minority students who major in sociology, and the number of
minority faculty members. Two PFF departments—at the University of
Nebraska, Lincoln, and at Texas A&M University—operate MOST programs.

Although the content of PFF programs varies from one institution to the
next, the components identified in this chapter are typical. PFF leaders report
that they make adjustments throughout the course of their programs to try to
meet the needs of all constituencies. The goal to have PFF programs become
integral components of doctoral education could not be realized in the two
years of this project, but all PFF program designs should include plans for sustainability.

# Chapter 4

# Disciplinary Society Activities and Reflections of Executives

*Only by changing both campus and disciplinary cultures will we succeed in our efforts to change graduate education.*

—James L. Applegate, past president, National Communication Association

The six collaborating social science and humanities disciplinary societies brought to this project a rich history of work on improving the preparation of future faculty as well as a tradition of promoting cutting-edge research. Their leadership in this project sends important signals that the national PFF initiative has broad support among faculty organizations and that it transcends any one discipline. Their major roles were to 1) select academic departments in their fields to innovate with PFF, 2) support, encourage, and assist these departments to develop successful PFF programs, 3) develop and disseminate resources that encourage more departments to develop programs, 4) promote PFF concepts as legitimate aspects of graduate education in the disciplines, and 5) infuse their disciplines with the PFF vision for preparing the next generation of faculty. This chapter discusses the societies' motivations for participating in this project, summarizes their PFF activities, and presents their perspectives on the PFF initiative.

## Why did the societies participate in this project?

There are many reasons why the preparation of doctoral students for the professoriate is a matter of concern to disciplinary societies. Traditionally, the societies have organized themselves to advance and highlight research in their fields—their annual meetings contain sessions on recent research findings, their journals publish the most intellectually significant research and theories, and their boards and committees typically consist largely of leading researchers, often from research universities. However, for at least two decades, the humanities and social science disciplinary societies currently involved in this project have recognized that supporting and disseminating research is not enough to serve the discipline adequately. Through various mechanisms, each of these societies also emphasizes the importance of teaching and learning, professional and career development of faculty members and graduate students, educational innovations, and knowledge of larger trends affecting higher education and the institutions in which their specializations are practiced. PFF affords these societies an additional opportunity to further these agendas within their organizations. The societies realize that doctoral students in their disciplines represent the society members of the future, and they recognize the importance of ensuring that the next generation of faculty be well-educated professionals.

Some societies, such as those in English and history, were attracted to PFF partly for the same reason that doctoral students and departments often are—the poor academic job market in their fields. But other disciplines, such as sociology and psychology, enjoy strong job markets and had other motivations. Leaders of all societies agree that PFF is about "fit"—the match between, on the one hand, the student's interests, skills, and values, and, on the other hand, the environment and expectations for faculty at different types of academic institutions. Research universities, however, often assume that doctoral students are likely to become faculty at other research institutions, and thus provide training in research but little in other areas. In reality, most academic jobs are in other types of institutions, and many new Ph.D.s are unprepared for such faculty positions as a result. And, for those who do obtain an academic position, many are not prepared for the realities they will encounter as new faculty, regardless of institutional type.

Disciplinary societies are aware of significant initiatives to improve under-graduate education and of the changing roles of faculty members. The societies perceive PFF as a strategy for enhancing doctoral education in ways that better prepare graduate students for and inform faculty of these changing realities.

By relating PFF to the challenges and opportunities facing the disciplines, the societies legitimized PFF ideas. They encouraged graduate faculty to look more carefully at the world of higher education in which new assistant profes-sors work. They called attention to the multiple roles of faculty, new approaches to teaching and learning, and innovations in undergraduate educa-tion. They also supported selected departments in their disciplines to imple-ment creative educational reforms so that programs would be more attuned to this changing world.

One other factor motivated the leaders of these societies to participate in this project: the opportunity to collaborate with other well-regarded organiza-tions. Most of the humanities and social science disciplinary society leaders knew each other well, and they respected one another. Collectively, the six soci-eties recognized that the need to better connect doctoral education to the expectations for new faculty justifies PFF innovations. Together, they achieved greater credibility than any one society could have. In addition, funding agen-cies perceived that supporting six societies collectively offered greater potential for national impact than supporting individual societies. This collaborative program also provided an opportunity for the disciplinary societies to partner with the Council of Graduate Schools (CGS) and the Association of American Colleges and Universities (AAC&U), two institutional membership groups. These partnerships provided a means for the societies to reach graduate deans, other institutional leaders, and other audiences, as well as to link disciplinary and institutional initiatives in new ways.

Faculty members and academic administrators may have perspectives of one another that are colored by campus dynamics. The PFF collaborations allowed the disciplinary societies representing faculty and the associations representing institutions to seek mutual understanding and create common support for the PFF initiative. PFF is an innovation that can be incorporated relatively easily into a department's doctoral program. It also represents a comfortable extension of the societies' historic values and activities. The PFF initiative is also aligned closely with the strategic missions of institutions to provide quality undergraduate education and to sustain the high quality of the educational enterprise and its responsiveness to the needs of constituents.

## What did the societies do?

Created a leadership team. Each society assembled a leadership team to provide oversight and support for the PFF initiative within the discipline. Society leaders headed the teams that included the chairs of key society committees or projects related to PFF, influential scholars, faculty members and doctoral students involved in PFF programs, and administrators and faculty members at primarily undergraduate institutions and community colleges. Each team provided advice on publicizing the PFF initiative and conducting a national competition for departments to develop model PFF programs.

With the active involvement of the leadership team, each society conducted a national competition in the winter and spring of 2000. As a result, the National Council of Teachers of English (NCTE) selected five departments for PFF awards and each of the other societies selected four. All are listed in Appendix II, along with their cluster institutions. In some cases, the leadership teams remained active throughout the project. For example, the American Sociological Association (ASA) team divided into two-member sub-teams, each of which conducted site visits and had continuing relationships with one cluster during the entire project.

**Connected PFF within the society.** In addition to forming leadership teams, societies connected PFF with related divisions and committees in their organizations. For example, the American Psychological Association (APA) Society of Teaching in Psychology appointed a task force to create a five-year plan for workshops on faculty development that included PFF among the program topics. These workshops were to be presented at annual meetings of the seven regional psychological associations. The American Political Science Association (APSA) connected PFF to its long-standing Departmental Services Program to inform political science department chairs at all types of colleges and universities about the attributes and outcomes of PFF. APSA also connected PFF with its Conference for Chairs by including PFF among conference agenda items. The National Communication Association (NCA) Educational Policies Board and its Doctoral Education Committee both support and connect to the association's PFF program.

**Supported the cluster programs.** The societies provided a good deal of assistance to the departmental leaders and cluster participants. They helped create opportunities for participants to network with colleagues from other clusters in their disciplines in order to share experiences, problems, and ideas. Mechanisms included the creation of listservs, as well as discussions at annual conferences and regional meetings at which chairs and leaders were encouraged to support PFF programs. The societies shared information with their members about the PFF Web site, which includes a growing knowledge base concerning PFF and resources for PFF programs, and distributed copies of PFF Occasional Papers. They also helped design and lead the 2001 and 2002 PFF summer working conferences that brought participants from all PFF departments together. These conferences provided opportunities for attendees to learn from each other, network, and discuss strategic issues facing the clusters, the disciplines, and the national PFF initiative.

Since there was broad agreement that the success of the PFF initiative requires sound empirical evidence, society executives also encouraged cluster leaders and their colleagues to participate in assessment efforts. Several discipline leaders or executives visited their clusters to learn first-hand how the PFF programs worked; to encourage the innovations; to meet personally with students, faculty members, and administrators; and to hear stories of what PFF meant to them. They also offered technical assistance and, in some cases, advised cluster leaders to make changes.

**Educated their members about PFF.** The design of PFF phase four called for disciplinary societies to communicate with members and educate them about PFF as part of their ongoing activities. The society executives led the efforts to promote PFF, both within the society and the leadership teams and among cluster leaders. The most common means of promoting PFF was through presentations of PFF activities by faculty and students at annual meeting sessions. For example, a session at the 2002 American Historical Association (AHA) annual meeting focused on two PFF history clusters and featured a faculty member from the graduate campus, a faculty member from a partner institution, and three doctoral students. The session was sponsored jointly by the AHA Teaching Division and the AHA Committee for Graduate Education.

Presentations by PFF students, partner faculty, and graduate faculty were included in all major NCTE conferences during the grant period, culminating in a full session devoted to each institutional cluster at the 2002 spring meeting.

At the 2001 APA annual convention, PFF-related activities included a pre-conference workshop for doctoral students and new faculty, a special forum for PFF students to share their experiences, and a faculty symposium.

Regional meetings of several participating disciplinary societies also incorporated programs on PFF. For example, NCA hosted a PFF presentation, followed by a reception, at each of four regional communication gatherings. The 2002 NCA program focused on the needs of students and was structured as a mini-PFF experience for doctoral students. Although regional sociology meetings are independent of ASA, several featured PFF sessions, which included participation by PFF students. A PFF session was held at the Midwest Political Science Association (MPSA) meeting in 2001; another session will be held at the 2003 MPSA meeting.

Each society also published information about PFF and PFF issues. NCA produced an attractive and informative brochure and a manual (National Communication Association 2002) on how to start PFF programs, both of which were adopted by other societies. Monthly magazines and society newsletters have also been vehicles for dissemination. For example, stories about PFF have been published in NCTE's quarterly newsletter, *The Council Chronicle*, NCA's monthly publication, *Spectra*, and APSA's newsletter for department chairs, "*For the Chair....*" ASA has produced four publications:

"Preparing Graduate Students to Teach," "Looking for a Job in a Teaching-Oriented Institution," "Taking Your First Job as an Assistant Professor," and "Proseminars in Sociology." APSA also hosted a symposium on PFF projects that was published in the December 2002 issue of *PS: Political Science and Politics.*

Each association developed a PFF Web presence. APA, for example, established a PFF-in-Psychology Web page as part of the APA Education Directorate website for graduate education and training (www.apa.org). That Web page links to psychology PFF program sites at the cluster institutions, as well as to the national PFF Web site. Thus, access is provided to a broad range of information about the purpose of PFF, various implementation models, and an extensive faculty development bibliography. APSA established an extensive Web page devoted to PFF (www.apsanet.org), which includes resources for PFF and related programs, significant research relating to student concerns about doctoral education, and descriptions of the missions of various colleges and universities.

Despite such attempts to educate members about the value and potential of PFF, Paul Bodmer of NCTE stated that PFF sessions in his discipline are not generally well attended. This reflects the difficulty of changing the culture of faculty preparation, even when the disciplinary societies are energetic advocates for PFF.

**Linked PFF to other activities.** The disciplinary societies embraced PFF because it was consistent with other disciplinary initiatives and could assist in accomplishing related society goals. For example, five of the societies—AHA, APA, APSA, ASA and NCA—connected PFF with the Scholarship of Teaching and Learning in the Disciplines program of the Carnegie Foundation for the Advancement of Teaching. APSA arranged a roundtable presentation at the 2001 conference entitled, "The Scholarship of Teaching and Learning in Political Science" (a transcript is included in the report of the symposium; Clarke, Hutchings, Keeter, Reeher, Alex-Assensoh 2002). NCA worked closely with the Carnegie Foundation to publish a monograph (Huber and Morreale 2002) highlighting the scholarship of teaching in ten disciplines.

As a result of its study of the role of Directors of Graduate Study (Subcommittee on Directors of Graduate Education, 1998), ASA decided to hold an annual meeting for individuals with these responsibilities. PFF was an agenda item for the first meeting, and departments were encouraged to develop such programs.

**Created programs to address underrepresentation of students of color.** Each of the societies has initiatives directed toward increasing the number of underrepresented faculty members in the discipline. Activities of the ASA are typical: supported by the National Institute of Mental Health, ASA sponsors the Minority Fellowship Program for pre-doctoral work in the sociology of mental health. ASA also includes among it activities PFF sessions for minority fellows who, like other fully funded students, have few opportunities to learn about faculty roles. Each of the four sociology PFF programs sent representatives to the Association of Black Sociologists' annual meeting to discuss the graduate student training opportunities available in their departments.

Indiana University, South Bend, a partner institution in the Indiana University cluster, engineered a temporary adjunct appointment at its campus for a minority doctoral student from Howard University who had completed all but the dissertation. This appointment is a win-win situation, integrating the appointee into the life of the department, providing her a year of exposure to an institution that is different from her home institution, and providing the faculty and students the opportunity to learn from a talented minority faculty member.

The social science and humanities disciplinary societies that participated in PFF see it as a disciplinary responsibility to improve the preparation of graduates for academic careers. And they are prepared to devote prominent and sustained attention, as well as resources, to this issue. But as Sheilah Mann of APSA observed, "We could never have [created the fourth phase of PFF] without the resources of a grant. Societies are not barriers to change, but they have limited ability to make change."

## What do disciplinary leaders see as the emergent outcomes?

Now, after three years of promoting PFF, society leaders sense the beginning of a cultural shift in doctoral education. Paul Nelson of APA observed that he especially valued conversations with graduate students during his visits to PFF clusters. One student told him: "We could never have had this conversation without PFF—it would have detracted from my research." This observation generated a vigorous discussion among the society executives that concluded, with many provisos, that a "paradigm shift" is taking place in graduate education. The discussion produced several other insights:

▲ Several years ago, surveys of departments asked what they did to help their graduate students learn to teach; now they ask what they do to prepare their graduate students more broadly. During this time of change, initial responses to new survey questions tended to be simplistic, but they have gradually become more sophisticated.

▲ If a paradigm shift is taking place, it is less evident at top-tier departments, where research is still enshrined as the only substantive requirement. Since many society board members are from such institutions, this poses a challenge to more general acceptance of change in the discipline.

▲ There are several examples of universities below the top-tier that are doing innovative things, suggesting a possible "bubble up" model of disciplinary change. Some question whether a "bubble up" strategy will actually lead to more general adoption of PFF, because top departments are unlikely to imitate programs at institutions outside their peer group.

There was greater agreement that PFF adds value for doctoral students, graduate programs, faculty and students in partner institutions, and the disciplines themselves. Each society has many anecdotes and stories that support these conclusions, but solid data will be needed to convince skeptics. As one society executive observed, "The opposite of anecdote is data." But as anecdotes accumulate, evidence starts to emerge of substantial positive outcomes of PFF—the forerunner of data that will develop over time.

The observations of two executives seem to capture the views of all disciplinary leaders. Carla Howery of ASA reflected that "PFF" suggests that we *prepare* future faculty, implying intentional action and assessment of how well that preparation works, which is in itself a breakthrough from standard practice. Graduate education usually involves a dyadic relationship between a student and an advisor. Even when that relationship works perfectly, a student can benefit more from the collective experiences and wisdom of the faculty than from simply the individual interactions that occur by taking classes or working with a research advisor. A collective approach to graduate education, such as a departmental PFF program, can improve mentoring of all students. PFF has set a new bar: students expect graduate programs to include preparation for a full range of career options, and hiring institutions rightly expect a faculty candidate to understand the nature of their institution and value its mission.

Paul Bodmer of NCTE reported that students in some of the English PFF programs gained an insight into campus politics when they were called upon to justify their program to the administration. Students in another English program felt a new sense of ownership when they were allowed to design some aspects of the PFF program to meet their needs. Most of the students he talked with felt their education was broadened significantly beyond what it would have been without the PFF program.

Perhaps the most important paradigm shift is that leaders of these disciplinary societies now view and discuss PFF not as a desirable "add-on," but as an essential part of preparation for work in the disciplines.

# Chapter 5

# Outcomes of PFF Programs

*PFF students felt that they knew more about the American academic scene and the variety of institutions that comprise it than their non-PFF competitors.... And they felt, almost to a person, that they knew better how to present themselves as professionals who could "fit" in different institutional environments.*
—Associate graduate dean who surveyed PFF alumni

What are the benefits of PFF programs for students? Are the outcomes the ones anticipated? What are the experiences and outcomes for faculty members and departments? The responses to these questions come from two sources: (1) student and faculty testimony on the value of PFF in preparing students for academic careers, and (2) the assessments of PFF that have been conducted over the decade of its existence. Collectively, these responses and assessments support a conclusion that PFF has been generally successful in meeting the intended goal of developing more effective preparation for faculty careers. The assessments also reveal a consensus among graduate deans, graduate and partner faculty, students, and alumni that the benefits to all who participate more than justify the effort required to establish and sustain the programs. This chapter provides evidence of the benefits to stakeholders. It also registers some concerns expressed by participants and revealed by the PFF assessments, and offers suggestions for addressing these.

Assessments of PFF include surveys of graduate student and faculty participants by PFF staff (Pruitt-Logan, Gaff, and Weibl 1998), case studies by program directors at the conclusion of the first phase of PFF, surveys and interviews with PFF alumni (DeNeef, 2002), surveys and observations by commissioned evaluators (Thomas 2002), and a focus group discussion by PFF doctoral students from different clusters (Millis 2002). The sponsors of the latest PFF phases, the National Science Foundation (NSF, phase three in the sciences and mathematics) and The Atlantic Philanthropies (AP, phase four in the humanities and the social sciences), have supported a three-year independent assessment of all phases of PFF. In addition, a great deal of information is available from other sources: electronic and other communications between Anne Pruitt-Logan and Jerry Gaff and PFF participants from many programs; visits by these authors to several PFF clusters; reports of the several summer working conferences involving teams from participating clusters; presentations by PFF participants at scores of professional meetings; and annual reports submitted by grantees. All of this information points to the conclusion that PFF has proven to be an effective approach to matching the purposes of doctoral education to the needs of hiring institutions. Most importantly, PFF responds to the professional aspirations of doctoral students, for whom PFF was conceptualized.

*PFF has proven to be an effective approach to matching the purposes of doctoral education to the needs of hiring institutions*

These conclusions are also supported by insights from several other studies of PFF programs (citations to specific studies will appear as each is discussed).

The messages from these experiences are presented primarily as quotes from reports of students and faculty, in an effort to convey their experiences accurately and in their own words.

## Views of PFF Directors and Deans

The views of PFF Directors and Deans are expressed in the results of the surveys of the NSF/AP assessment of PFF. Between December 2001 and March 2002, sixty-five of sixty-seven program directors and thirty-three of fifty-nine graduate deans completed questionnaires as part of this assessment. In spring 2002, approximately 400 graduate and 450 partner faculty were surveyed. The assessment also included visits by evaluators to several of the PFF campus project sites and interviews with participants. During the fall 2002 semester, approximately 4,000 graduate student "core participants" in PFF were surveyed. On July 15, 2002, NSF/AP released preliminary findings of the completed activities to the Council of Graduate Schools and the Association of American Colleges and Universities for the sole purpose of providing information to those wishing to plan new or to improve existing PFF programs.

These preliminary results indicate that, collectively, 97 percent of PFF directors and graduate deans believed the PFF programs at their institutions were "very successful" or "somewhat successful." Respondents were asked to name the elements that contributed most to the success of their programs. Here are some of their answers.

▲  "The combination of graduate students who see the need for PFF activities in their preparation and energetic faculty members who have taken the lead in providing them, is a self-motivating, self-propelling kind of synergy."

▲ "Students really like the interdisciplinary discussions and emphasis on diversity throughout our seminar series."

▲ "Our program promotes graduate student interaction, autonomy, and self-development. Individuals who emerge from the process are better able to act on and talk about their futures as scholars, teachers, and faculty members."

▲ "Our students have at least two full-fledged mentorships during PFF. Our partner faculty have been very high quality. Many of them have had students every year or even every semester for five years."

▲ "The program conveys to students that they are being prepared to be professionals in the full sense of the term."

▲ [The most important aspects included] "support from chair, graduate dean, and provost; enthusiasm of several of the students involved in the program; and cooperation with partners to make [PFF] a reciprocal, mutually beneficial arrangement."

▲ "The fact that PFF activities are a formal, required part of our program, and not add-ons."

At the time the fourth phase of PFF was launched, it was thought that PFF might be more eagerly embraced by faculty in the social sciences and humanities than by those in the physical and life sciences and mathematics disciplines. However, project directors and deans across all disciplines report that graduate faculty who become acquainted with the goals and outcomes of PFF are generally positive. Greater support for PFF may exist in the humanities and social sciences because a larger percentage of Ph.D. graduates in these disciplines are employed as faculty members. While upwards of 75 percent of humanities and 67 percent of social science Ph.D. graduates typically pursue academic careers, approximately 75 percent of doctoral graduates in chemistry, for example, take positions outside the academy (Ingram and Brown 1997). Thus, chemistry graduate faculty may see less value in providing special programs for the relatively few graduates who seek academic careers.

Support may also result from the belief that PFF experiences may enhance a student's chances of obtaining an academic job in the areas of the social sciences and humanities, where fewer jobs are available. Thus, more social science and humanities students were likely to see as useful the kind of preparation provided by PFF programs.

Another reason for greater support for PFF in the social science and humanities could be that the disciplinary societies in those fields have long emphasized pedagogy and professional development. Similarly, PFF may complement pre-existing programs of research into education, student learning, and the teaching profession within the humanities and social science disciplines.

In addition, faculty in different disciplines may differ about how closely graduate students should work with and be mentored by partner faculty. Eighty-two percent of PFF directors indicate that graduate students in PFF programs work closely with faculty at partner institutions, although participation of partner faculty is significantly higher in the social sciences and humanities than in the physical sciences and mathematics.

Eighty-two percent of directors from all disciplines report that PFF sessions at conferences or meetings had either a significant or limited impact. Sixty-eight percent indicated that society newsletter accounts of PFF had an impact in the discipline. The directors of humanities and social science programs report a higher impact and visibility in their disciplines than do directors of mathematics and science programs.

For these and perhaps other reasons that may vary from discipline to discipline, PFF has found a particularly sympathetic home among the humanities and social sciences.

## Assessments Conducted by Clusters

Although the PFF programs in the humanities and social sciences have operated for only two years, several clusters have begun the process of assessing results, and what they are learning is enlightening. "Our graduate students' response to the program has been very positive," reports Richard Simpson, a political science professor at the University of Illinois at Chicago. "Our students have been uniformly positive in their formal, written evaluations of the PFF courses." He also reports: "Since we instituted the PFF program, [the evaluations of our teaching assistants] have dramatically improved. One of the important outcomes has been that we as a department are doing a better job of teaching our undergraduate, not just our graduate, students."

Although there is broad agreement that additional quantitative assessments of PFF programs are needed, qualitative assessments have also been found to be important, especially for improving cluster programs. For example, each student in the psychology PFF program at Miami University of Ohio prepares a short reflective essay on his or her PFF experiences, and the department conducts focus groups with various constituencies. These qualitative approaches have been much more helpful and informative than initial quantitative evaluation instruments. According to faculty director Cecilia Shore, "The most common aspect of [students'] reflections [is] how much they have learned about the diversity of student needs at different institutions and about the flexibility they need as teachers to respond to those needs." Almost as often, students mention becoming aware of faculty roles in different institutions, and they are grateful to partner faculty mentors for helping them develop these insights. She continues: "Their reflections indicate that the [PFF] program has helped them in making career decisions, and has also been helpful in learning job search skills."

Students in the psychology department at the University of New Hampshire have participated in the university-wide PFF program for several years, and the department documents their skills and competencies. Students routinely develop a portfolio of their accomplishments in teaching, research, and service. The students also identify the experiences that contributed to the development of specific competencies. In addition, the department tracks its graduates, maintains accurate, up-to-date career records, and periodically surveys its PFF alumni. The department has carried out extensive assessment of a similar program

*Sudents mention becoming aware of faculty roles in different institutions, and they are grateful to partner faculty mentors for helping them develop these insights.*

that had operated for 35 years, until 1998, when their PFF program was established. Benassi and Fernald (1993) reported that introductory psychology students gave comparable evaluations to doctoral students and graduate faculty who taught the same course. Because surveys revealed that their psychology Ph.D. alumni spend about 60 percent of their time in teaching-related work, the department's graduate program has placed greater emphasis on preparation for teaching. When the psychology Ph.D. alumni were asked to rank ten program components in order of importance to their development as psychologists, they listed the top four as the course on the teaching of psychology, relationships with faculty, the dissertation, and the opportunity to teach their own course(s).

Many disciplines stress placement records as a measure of PFF success, and departments are urged to maintain placement records and contact information for all Ph.D. graduates and to survey alumni about the effectiveness of their graduate program. One way to judge success of a PFF program is to compare the placement rate of PFF graduates to department graduates who did not participate in PFF. By this measure, Florida State University's PFF program in history has been extraordinarily successful. Since the department joined PFF in 1998, it has awarded 37 Ph.D. degrees and 19 of these graduates are employed in tenure track positions, including all six of the department's PFF participants.

Another measure of placement success is whether graduates are well prepared for academic positions in non-research institutions. Indiana University has a highly-ranked department of sociology, and three of its recent PFF graduates are now faculty members at McDaniel College.

Placement is an important measure, but it reflects only one aspect of success. Comments from PFF graduates and alumni (including some who did not participate in PFF) have been extremely useful to program directors in securing broader faculty support for their PFF program. Moreover, there is general agreement that placement may be a more important measure of success in some disciplines than in others. For instance, some disciplines (such as sociology) have very little trouble placing graduates who desire academic jobs, and in these disciplines, placement is less important than other aspects of PFF in defining the success and value of the program. Measuring success of PFF requires that multiple forms of assessment be employed, including such tools as "exit interviews," focus groups, teaching evaluations, and surveys of alumni.

PFF programs in these humanities and social science departments are too young for assessments to provide conclusive evidence of their success, but evidence is accumulating that reinforces earlier data.

## Views of Graduate Students

Several studies of PFF programs completed over the last decade offer insights into various aspects of the PFF student experience. For example, these studies have identified reasons students choose to participate in PFF and the benefits they realize from participating. Students are also candid about their perceived obstacles to participation.

### Motives and expectations of students who participate

Doctoral students are drawn to the PFF program for a variety of reasons (Pruitt-Logan, Gaff, and Weibl 1998):

▲ To explore the possibility of a faculty career and learn about faculty roles;

▲ To enhance their teaching skills and learn from a teaching mentor;

▲ To learn about institutions with missions, student bodies, and expectations for faculty that differ from those of the research universities where they are pursuing their doctoral degree;

▲ To earn a "credential" that will help them secure an academic job; and

▲ To learn about the academic profession that they expect to enter.

Studies of student experiences in PFF programs in the social sciences and humanities, as well as conversations that program directors had with participating students, mirror the results of the assessment of an earlier phase of PFF. In an assessment of the science and mathematics phase, 95 percent of PFF graduate student respondents indicated that the programs either met or exceeded their expectations (Thomas 2002).

## Benefits to students from participating in PFF

From the beginning, doctoral students have reported an array of benefits from their PFF programs:

▲ **Learning about faculty roles and activities**

A PFF student in English at Michigan Technological University spoke for many when she attested to the value of learning about faculty life while still in graduate school:

"When a graduate student is making the transition to the new identity of a faculty member, she might think of herself as something of an ethnographer, observing a culture to gain insight not only about working conditions and departmental politics, but also about such things as how the institution operates, its history, what issues are still at stake, and who constitutes the various positions on particular issues. These are insights that novice faculty members sometimes can't determine until they're well into the tenure process, and having an opportunity to investigate institutions on the terms we PFF [participants] had, was rich indeed." This student testifies to one of the important benefits of PFF programs, which is to involve students in the "politics" of the profession.

One sociology student at Indiana University put it this way: "PFF has shown me that teaching, research, and service are not discrete entities but that the lines are constantly blurred. You can actively blur the line and have a much more fulfilling academic career, and PFF has definitely shown me how I can do that."

▲ **Developing expertise as a teacher, articulating a teaching philosophy, and using different approaches to engage students**

A student in psychology at the University of Georgia observed that: "Institutions are placing greater emphasis on teaching and learning competencies as well as issues of civic engagement. PFF is helping me prepare for the increasingly important role as teacher, and I am developing a professional identity that is not solely research- or practice-focused."

▲ **Understanding the variety of institutions in which graduates may work and the expectations those institutions have for their faculty**

A communication and culture student from Indiana University stated: "The most important thing … in terms of teaching and learning has been a sense of what the expectations are at different types of institutions, which is something I hadn't really considered prior to PFF. That was really important in giving me a sense of diversity of institutions and the different emphases they place on teaching."

▲ **Being mentored by a faculty member at a partner institution**

Faculty at partner institutions often serve as non-research mentors to PFF students, providing advice and serving as role models in curriculum development, classroom presentation, and technology-based learning. Some have co-authored teaching-related work with PFF students. And their advice is exempt from the "power factor" that exists in the student's graduate department between faculty and graduate students.

▲ **Developing a network of professional colleagues who can assist in job searches**

"PFF has provided opportunities for me," said a psychology student at Miami University of Ohio. She reported that she met people from the AAC&U and the Council of Graduate Schools, toured the APA offices, and "was exposed to…wonderful resources" that neither she nor other students had been aware of before.

▲ **Increasing students' sense of self-confidence as academic professionals**

A University of South Florida English student put it this way: "Too often graduate education focuses mainly on the scholarly aspect of academic life while ignoring the fact that the majority of the professional life of a scholar will probably be spent teaching, working on committees, [doing] administration, and the like. PFF has provided a much broader academic experience that I believe has more fully prepared me for the realities of an academic career."

▲ **Empowering students for the job-market**

One of the most frequently reported benefits of participating in a PFF program is that it empowers students by making intangibles tangible and by turning what sometimes appear as the vagaries of the academic job market into a much more deliberate process. A newly-minted Ph.D. in political science who participated in the University of Colorado— Stanford PFF program commented on the impact of PFF on his search for an academic position: "Having participated in PFF, I was better able to convey in interviews that I had a vision of the life I would lead [as a faculty member], and that I had definite plans for fulfilling my research agenda while being a good teacher and university citizen. And the faculty were reassured that I had a realistic map for navigating the road to tenure."

A sociology student from the University of Nebraska-Lincoln stated: "PFF gave me a faster start in my faculty job [at a small liberal arts college]. I had a teaching portfolio and several courses sketched out, and I understood that I would be put on committees. I was mentally prepared [for these responsibilities] from my time shadowing a faculty member at a similar college [as a PFF student]."

▲  **Clarifying students' career choices**

Some students find that their career goals change as a result of participating in PFF; others find their goals reinforced. A psychology student at the University of Colorado expressed it this way: "PFF hasn't really affected the direction of my career goals, but it has sharpened them .... I am stronger in my resolve because I am more realistic about what lies before me."

A communication student at Indiana University summarized this benefit: "Not only has the PFF program taught me 'how' to become a professor, it also has assured me that this is the right profession for me."

A sociology student from Texas A&M University stated: "I had stereotypes about the students and faculty at community colleges. Through my PFF experience at a community college, I was [overwhelmed] by the wonderful teaching, outstanding technology tools, the eager first-generation students, the small classes, and the satisfaction of the faculty. I changed my mind about the kind of job I would seek."

## Growing Recognition of PFF

**At the national level:** The American Association for Higher Education offers full support for graduate students to attend its national conference through its K. Patricia Cross Future Leaders Award. Criteria for selection include potential for leadership in teaching and learning, a strong sense of civic responsibility, and a commitment to contribute to others as leaders, scholars, and citizens—all values emphasized in PFF programs. In 2002, PFF students represented three of the seven selected: Ingrid Hoffman in child psychology at the University of Minnesota, Julio Rojas in psychology at the University of Georgia, and Camilla Saulsbury in sociology at Indiana University.

The Indiana University Department of Sociology won the Distinguished Contribution to Teaching Award of the ASA for its PFF program and excellence in teacher preparation—a signal honor for a top-ranked research department that happily blurs the lines between teaching and research.

**At the state level:** Connie Mixon, a former PFF student and now a tenured political science faculty member at Richard J. Daley Community College in Chicago, was recognized as the Carnegie Foundation for the Advancement of Teaching "Illinois Teacher of the Year" in 2002.

**At the local level:** The Faculty Women's Association at ASU sponsors awards for achievements in scholarship, research, and leadership. Since 1995, eight of the seventeen recipients have been PFF students or alumni. (Marjorie Zatz, Associate Dean of the Graduate College, 2002, personal communication).

## Challenges and Recommendations for Improving the Experience of PFF Students

Graduate students are the primary beneficiaries of PFF and are among its most ardent supporters. However, students also experience challenges and perceive obstacles that inhibit their full participation in PFF. The most frequent are:

▲ The time required to take classes, attend workshops and other PFF activities, and to visit and hold internships at partner campuses;

▲ The perception that students encounter among graduate faculty that PFF participation may distract from research; and

▲ The complexity of logistics and travel to partner institutions.

The collective experience over all phases of PFF provides some guidance on how these concerns can be addressed.

## 1. Time-management

Students cite concerns about time-management as the greatest challenge to participation in PFF. In particular, they worry about the time required to take courses, attend workshops, and visit other campuses. A related concern is that a menu of PFF activities is often presented to new students, with little guidance as to how to fit those activities into the student's own graduate program or how to select those that best fit with the students' educational objectives. The time required to participate in PFF activities depends in part on the structure and flexibility of the program. These concerns have been addressed primarily either through flexible scheduling of PFF activities or through creating a "developmentally structured" program of PFF activities.

Flexible scheduling of PFF events has helped mitigate time concerns in some programs by scheduling activities at times that minimize overlap with research, teaching, or departmental activities. Thus, PFF courses, workshops, and seminars may be offered late in the day, especially Friday afternoon, on weekends, or during lunch periods. At other times, activities may be scheduled to precede or follow departmental seminars or other departmental events. Such activities may allow PFF students to engage the topic of the seminar or event from the perspectives related to faculty work, pedagogy, or student learning. For example, a history department seminar revealing new aspects of world history might be used as the basis for a PFF session on how one might incorporate such new scholarship into history courses for undergraduate students, or how a faculty member might create opportunities for undergraduate students to participate in research that expands on that presented in the seminar.

Students who participate in PFF often serve as peer mentors to newer participants, plan and coordinate PFF activities, and provide leadership in many other ways. Arizona State University's history PFF program has found that rotating leadership among participating students helped alleviate time concerns of some prospective participants, while allowing for the fresh perspectives of new people.

Developmental PFF programs are structured so that activities are integrated into the graduate curriculum and match the various stages of a student's graduate course of study. Some programs find that this approach addresses time-management problems in a way that better meets the needs of students and the cluster than a menu of PFF options.

Professional development is an important aspect of preparation for a career, and new graduate students should be made aware early in their program of the opportunities afforded by PFF. An early PFF orientation workshop engages students in consideration of the issue of professional development at a time when the benefits may not be readily apparent. "Raising student awareness of professional development issues before they are on the job market remains a major challenge," says Jonathan Grant, history PFF director at Florida State University, who recommends that departments introduce all new graduate students to the PFF program from their first day of department orientation. Others concur that such early exposure creates a "habit of mind" among doctoral candidates to search out a variety of professional development opportunities in research, teaching, and service throughout their graduate program. While students are expected to take an entrepreneurial approach toward pursuing professional development opportunities, PFF programs can make these opportunities more accessible to students by integrating them into the graduate program.

A developmentally structured PFF program might, for example, offer students opportunities to participate in courses, seminars, or workshops on:

▲ "Teaching the Discipline" before their first TA assignment;
▲ Professional ethics and mentoring before working with partner faculty; and
▲ Job search strategies as they prepare to enter the job market.

Including partner faculty in PFF activities at the anchor institution is important for students. They acquire confidence through interacting with partner faculty in activities at their home institution and thereby take better advantage of these mentors at the partner campus.

Whether cluster needs are met with flexible scheduling or with a developmental structure, PFF is most successful when it is an integral part of the graduate program. The result of such integration is that students perceive PFF activities, not as competing with other degree requirements such as comprehensive exams and research, but rather as important components of the total graduate experience.

## 2. PFF and Research Responsibilities

There is, of course, a real concern and a realistic possibility that PFF participation could lengthen the time to degree. Disciplinary leaders, however, believe this is not the central issue in the humanities and social sciences. In fact, they feel that PFF participation may focus a student's work and actually shorten the time to degree. A more serious issue is that PFF participation may detract from students' research efforts. This may be true in the social sciences and humanities, even though research on professional socialization and the history of the discipline, as well as on learning assessment strategies, are often integral parts of the graduate curriculum. A number of institutional clusters have found innovative ways to integrate research on teaching and learning in the discipline into PFF programs. For example, graduate students in the sociology PFF program at the University of Nebraska, Lincoln, create a "Scholarship of Teaching and Learning" project in which they learn about classroom-based research and evaluation. This program is structured so that students carry the research and teaching skills developed in the first phase of the project into a second phase involving a partner faculty mentor. Drawing from the work of Cross, Angelo, and Steadman (Cross and Steadman 1996; Angelo and Cross 1993), this aspect of the program challenges traditional distinctions between research and teaching. As John Reilly, program director of English PFF at Howard University, emphasizes, it is important to make clear that teaching is researchable, and that all of the work that faculty perform is subject to rational inquiry, theory, and evaluation. When graduate education embraces this fact, everyone benefits: faculty, students, the discipline, and society.

Robert Johnson, director of the English PFF program at Michigan Technological University, believes that humanities graduate students require a flexible PFF model that is open to exploring research opportunities, as well as enhanced teaching and service experiences. As he explains, "Humanities departments have long trained graduate students in teaching methods. We might think about [humanities PFF programs as] encouraging research—kind of turning the tables on the science and engineering PFF programs." As PFF program directors continue to tailor PFF to the needs of their particular discipline, research components relating to the scholarship of teaching and learning may become more prominent.

## 3. Complexity of Travel and Logistics

Another frequent concern of students regards arrangements and logistics associated with travel to partner institutions. Although some programs have indicated they have the resources to include even international partners and provide opportunities for their students to teach abroad, it is more typical that even relatively short commutes pose difficulties for students. PFF programs provide organizational support to students and faculty to help form working relationships with partner faculty. Arizona State University's Graduate College assigns a graduate student to coordinate work with clusters and to assist students with travel arrangements. Other programs organize group visits to partner campuses and orientation sessions to facilitate student-mentor relationships. Many PFF program leaders and students assert that conferences and disciplinary society meetings serve to address travel difficulties and to provide alternate venues for networking. As Susan Clarke, the PFF director in political science at the University of Colorado, describes: "Even the 30 miles between Denver and Boulder or the scenic 90-minute trip to Colorado Springs [presented] logistical hazards in the midst of the semester." The University of Colorado-Stanford University cluster discovered that national PFF conferences and PFF sessions at APSA meetings "proved to be key opportunities [for students and faculty] to spend time with each other and to meet faculty and students in other PFF-like programs."

Students in PFF programs also express the need for earlier and more frequent information on career options for program graduates. They also want more opportunities for job skills development and assistance with job search strategies and placement. These issues and concerns are not specific to PFF participants; they are common to all graduate students. PFF cluster leaders report that PFF programs provide ideal forums for meeting the common needs and concerns of graduate students.

## Views of Alumni

In the two years since PFF programs in the social sciences and humanities were initiated, only a small number of doctoral students have received their degrees and secured academic appointments. Therefore, systematic research has not yet been conducted on this group. However, the PFF National Office commissioned a survey of the impact of PFF upon the careers of alumni from previous phases who hold faculty positions (DeNeef 2002). This group includes alumni in the social sciences and humanities as well as in the sciences and mathematics. Of 271 alumni contacted, 129 responded. Twenty-five respondents were subsequently interviewed by telephone. The survey results revealed that PFF made a difference in the experiences of these individuals in three primary ways.

▲ Alumni believe their doctoral student experience was qualitatively different—and better—than it would have been had they not participated in PFF.

▲ They believe that PFF experiences aided them in their job searches, and they typically cited PFF as a central reason for their job offers.

▲ They report that what they learned through PFF helped them get a faster and surer start as new faculty members than their faculty peers.

One of the more interesting of DeNeef's findings is that PFF alumni commonly serve as resources for their new faculty colleagues. For example, Wendy Crone, a new faculty member in engineering at the University of Wisconsin, Madison, reports: "PFF provided me with a basket of tools that I am still trying out, tools that I can pick and choose from as the need arises." Because of this "basket of tools," Crone's peers are seeking her advice on various professional matters. "I have become a *de facto* mentor to my colleagues," she observed (DeNeef, p. 16).

DeNeef's findings are supported by anecdotal evidence from other PFF alumni, who consistently report that PFF enriched the quality of their graduate school experience, improved their job search skills, helped them obtain a faculty position, and allowed them to hit the ground running.

## Views of Faculty Members

Throughout all phases of PFF, both graduate faculty and faculty from partner institutions have consistently reported a range of benefits from their participation in PFF programs and activities. Likewise, departments with PFF programs report a consistent set of benefits from having a departmental PFF program (Pruitt-Logan, Gaff, and Weibl 1998).

## Benefits to graduate faculty from participating in PFF

Benefits commonly reported by graduate faculty include:

▲ A deeper understanding of the roles and responsibilities of faculty members at various institutions;

▲ The opportunity to get to know some students quite well, to share ideas about teaching and academic careers, and to learn from them;

▲ A better understanding of and communication with participating students, which also helped departments identify areas of their graduate program that needed attention;

▲ The opportunity to become acquainted with colleagues at other institutions; and

▲ An appreciation for their students' increasingly sophisticated understanding of faculty roles and responsibilities.

One graduate faculty member testified, with the pride all good teachers and mentors take in the success of their students: "One of my senior doctoral students has just become the first successful faculty placement from our PFF program." Melbourne Cummings, PFF cluster leader in the communications and culture department at Howard University, summarizes the perspectives of PFF graduate faculty: "The PFF program is deeply embedded in our department's academic program. Our PFF students are constantly involved with faculty, both at Howard and our partner institutions. And faculty and administrators across the campus are excited about the opportunity PFF affords for them to share their views and expertise with students preparing to be faculty members." These views cover faculty governance, diversity in the classroom and workplace, effective teaching strategies and learning assessment tools, and professional ethics and responsibilities.

## Benefits to partner faculty from participating in PFF

Many partner faculty choose to participate in PFF out of a combination of good will and a professional sense of responsibility to the discipline. Partner faculty who participated in the humanities and social science PFF projects report a number of benefits similar to those reported by faculty in previous surveys and phases of the program. Most of the phase four PFF partner faculty had no previous occasion to work with advanced and energetic doctoral students, and they appreciated this opportunity. Many report that they appreciated the feedback on their own teaching from the PFF graduate students. And partner faculty appreciated receiving recognition for their participation.

*Many partner faculty choose to participate in PFF out of a combination of good will and a professional sense of responsibility the discipline*

For example, the Arizona State University (ASU) history department recognizes the participation of partner faculty through such benefits as free library privileges, free internet access, and special parking rates on the ASU campus. Such concrete forms of recognition foster a formal connection to the culture of the doctoral institution that partner faculty value.

Other specific benefits frequently mentioned by partner faculty include:

▲ Ideas for improving their teaching, scholarship, and community service;

▲ The benefit to their undergraduate students of learning from PFF graduate students about topics not typically included in the curriculum;

▲ The advice PFF graduate students give their undergraduate students about applying to and succeeding in graduate programs;

▲ The contact and development of strong ties with faculty peers from other institutions;

▲ The potential for PFF graduate students to serve as additional faculty resources for the department, in capacities such as adjunct faculty or sabbatical replacements;

▲ The satisfaction of helping to prepare future members of the professoriate;

▲ The opportunity to give PFF graduate students the mentoring experiences that they themselves did not have; and

▲ Insight into the ever-changing needs of the discipline.

Many faculty participants echo the comment of Carolyn Calhoon-Dilahunt, an English instructor at Yakima Valley Community College, a partner of Washington State University: "It has been an interesting experience to get a cross-disciplinary, cross-institutional view of higher education. I have learned a lot about our cluster and how each of our institutions functions, of course, but I [also] have a better understanding of what is happening in higher education and differences of institutions and of disciplines across the nation."

Both graduate and partner faculty report that they are energized and revitalized by working with PFF students and reconnecting with the roots of their own interests in an academic career. Graduate and partner faculty often envision themselves as inhabiting different worlds, and they see PFF as a way to bridge those worlds. Oneida Meranto, a partner faculty member in political science at Metropolitan State College of Denver, remarked that participation in PFF "prevents our department from developing feelings of isolation within the discipline—it helps keep us informed."

## Enhancing the faculty experience of participating in PFF

Faculty members who participate in PFF are generally quite enthusiastic in their overall assessment of their experiences. However, both anchor and partner faculty express some concerns that revolve around three issues:

▲ The time-commitment required to participate in PFF
▲ Clear communication concerning the nature and expectations of faculty involvement in PFF
▲ Rewards and recognition for participating in PFF

Graduate and partner faculty generally have a full load of teaching and service responsibilities and are concerned that participation in PFF will simply add to an already full load. Because most faculty did not have PFF experience in their graduate education, they may have little basis for understanding the nature and goals of such a program and how they can contribute to it. Faculty also have a concern that their work in PFF will not be recognized as a legitimate component of their effort. Some faculty may fear that their participation will limit the time and effort for research and other faculty activities that are more commonly recognized and rewarded.

Faculty who direct PFF programs should communicate frequently and articulate clearly the purpose and benefits of faculty participation. PFF programs are often initiated by only one or a few department faculty members. However, if PFF is to evolve into an integral part of a department's graduate program, there must be acceptance, if not active involvement, of many faculty. Frequent information to department faculty about PFF activities and accomplishments is required to build a foundation of support for a broader departmental embrace of PFF concepts and activities.

Partner faculty need to feel integrated into the overall PFF program from the outset. They should be fully apprised of the program schedule, including changes such as a delay in the arrival of PFF students on their campus for mentoring. PFF programs also benefit from including partner faculty in other activities on the anchor campus, such as orientation sessions and activities that will relate to students' work on the partner campus.

PFF program directors also make several recommendations to address faculty concerns:

▲  Reward faculty with release time from other duties to participate in PFF or recognize PFF involvement as part of their instructional or service responsibilities.

▲  Provide small stipends or flexible funds to faculty who participate in PFF.

▲  Assist faculty in arranging mentoring opportunities and PFF activities.

## Benefits to departments from incorporating PFF as a component of the graduate program

Both students and faculty suggested that a PFF program increases the perceived quality of a department. A department that demonstrates a concern about students' potential academic careers, offers a thoughtful program to prepare students for the variety of such careers that exist, and creates opportunities for students to learn about the profession through close relationships with talented mentors, is likely to be perceived as being of high-quality by students as well as colleagues.

Faculty members and doctoral students who participate in PFF are almost always enthusiastic about their PFF experience, and departments benefit from satisfied faculty and students.

Some doctoral programs have found PFF to be a useful recruiting tool, and there is anecdotal evidence that PFF attracts high-quality students to a graduate program.

According to Ronald Lee, a professor in the communication studies department at the University of Nebraska-Lincoln, "PFF is becoming an important recruitment tool. … [Prospective] students are eager to talk about PFF and are comforted by the thought that the faculty is thinking about their professional success from the moment they enter [our graduate program]." (Lee 2001).

The PFF National Office often receives inquiries from students who wish to participate in PFF. One typical example is a query from a student completing a master's degree in sociology requesting information on doctoral sociology departments that have PFF programs.

The humanities and social science departments participating in this fourth phase of PFF have had only two years to design and implement these new programs—not nearly enough time to assess the value of the programs to participants or to employ those assessments as recruiting aids. However, institutions such as the University of New Hampshire and Howard University that established PFF programs in previous phases have found PFF to be useful in recruiting high-quality doctoral students.

PFF students consistently report that they are able to navigate the job search more effectively than their peers without PFF experience. This suggests that graduates of a department with a PFF program have a competitive advantage in their initial academic job search.

A National Communication Association brochure (2001) summarizes the benefits of PFF for communication doctoral programs:

▲  PFF enriches the doctoral education experience.
▲  PFF creates a sense of community in the department.
▲  PFF aids in the recruitment, retention, and marketability of doctoral students.
▲  PFF helps build alliances and support within the university.
▲  PFF helps establish regional disciplinary collaborations with partner faculty.

The anecdotal and other evidence discussed above supports the view that providing opportunities such as PFF is the right thing to do. Thus, there is a basis for concluding that a PFF program can raise the reputation of a department's graduate program while improving the undergraduate education in both anchor and partner institutions.

## Benefits for the discipline

In addition to the benefits that students, faculty, and departments attribute to PFF program participation, leaders of the disciplinary societies involved in this project assert that PFF also accrues benefits to the academic disciplines themselves. Carla Howery of ASA includes among these: attracting new members— both graduate students and partner faculty; enriching the disciplinary society and its annual meetings through new work and topics—PFF students have revealed some new teaching facets that were "real gems"; and fostering "cross-talk" on important issues such as graduate training, which helps improve the practice throughout the discipline.

In cases where there is no disciplinary-based state organization to provide opportunities for members of the discipline to meet, the PFF clusters have provided an essential means to foster professional ties among scholars. In addition, beyond the immediate purpose of preparing Ph.D. graduates to succeed in faculty positions, PFF participants report that cluster activities foster a stronger sense of their professional identity within and responsibility for stewardship of the discipline. For example, the PFF clusters in communication worked with leaders of the NCA to plan and offer a workshop on survival skills for doctoral students at the NCA National Convention. Although the workshop originated with the PFF clusters, it was open to all student attendees. Workshop participants received a certificate identifying them as a "steward of the communication discipline." All PFF students who attended were expected to make a public presentation of their workshop experience at their home campuses. This important additional role of developing a sense of professionalism and responsibility for the discipline results from engaging all stakeholders to reflect on professional roles and responsibilities in a larger context, beyond the bounds of graduate education.

# Chapter 6

# Challenges for the Future: Changing the Culture of Faculty Preparation

*I think it's important to change the paradigm when
we think about faculty positions and change the pedagogy
when we think about teaching....*

—Graduate Student in Sociology, Texas A&M University

This chapter takes a forward look at sustaining PFF programs and envisioning their future within the context of many other initiatives with similar objectives.

It is important to recall the context in which the Preparing Future Faculty initiative was launched: a confluence of studies and testimony from students and faculty suggesting changes in doctoral education that would be beneficial to graduates and employers. Specifically, there was strong support for the notion that new faculty should be prepared for the many roles and expectations of faculty across the spectrum of hiring institutions. A sizeable majority of Ph.D. graduates who pursue a faculty career will do so at an institution that is different in many ways from their doctoral university. These hiring institutions see a broader preparation of faculty as an essential strategy for improving the education of undergraduate students. This was an important factor in the decision of The Atlantic Philanthropies to support PFF programs in the humanities and social sciences as well as of the NSF to support science and mathematics PFF programs.

# Integrating PFF into Doctoral Education

Higher education has a long history of educational innovations that emerge, gain widespread attention, and then disappear from the landscape, especially if they are dependent on external funding. A major challenge for PFF is to sustain the significant number of departmental and university-wide programs that currently exist across the disciplines. Although the humanities and social science disciplines have provided a receptive environment, they also face special challenges. These disciplines are related intellectually in ways that augur well for synergy. Larger numbers of programs will be required, however, to effect systemic change in the culture of graduate education in these disciplines. This fourth phase of PFF included six disciplinary societies, each of which created four or five experimental PFF programs that have operated for only two years. These departments represent less than 10 percent of doctoral departments in any of these disciplines, and these departmental programs have operated for less than one-half of the average time required to complete a Ph.D. degree (Hoffer, *et al.* 2002). Much more time will be needed to produce Ph.D. graduates who demonstrate by their successful faculty careers the benefit of PFF to students and to departments. In the humanities and social sciences alone, many more departmental programs with similarly well-documented results will be needed to change the "culture of preparation" of faculty. Effecting change throughout such a large, complex, and decentralized enterprise as doctoral education is a far greater and longer-term undertaking.

Three strategic actions will be required to integrate PFF into doctoral "education:

▲ Establish collective responsibility for doctoral education;
▲ Clearly articulate the collective benefits of PFF; and
▲ Secure administrative support for PFF.

Each of these actions is expanded upon below.

## Establishing collective responsibility for graduate education

In theory, doctoral education is conceived to be the collective responsibility of graduate faculty in the department or program offering the degree. In practice, the responsibility is often assumed by the research mentor, and the dyadic relationship between doctoral student and research mentor is the primary aspect of the student's graduate experience. One of the goals of PFF is to move graduate education toward a more collective endeavor of members of a department or program faculty and others (such as faculty at partner institutions) who can be effective mentors for preparing students for the total array of expectations of faculty members. The disciplinary societies that represent faculty professional interests are seen as key players in building this broader consensus among faculty for changing doctoral education.

The leaders of the social science and humanities disciplinary societies that created programs in this fourth phase of PFF plan to continue their support for the program. They believe that the disciplines have a responsibility to improve the preparation of new faculty members for an academic career, and that this issue requires the societies' prominent and sustained attention. The societies can leverage their influence by partnering with educational associations and departments willing to experiment with innovative practices.

## Articulating the benefits of PFF

The graduates of PFF programs who are now in faculty positions are especially articulate spokespersons for the student benefits of PFF and ardent promoters of PFF concepts. As PFF programs take firmer hold in departments and the number of programs grows, there will be increasing numbers of alumni who will be in various stages of their own academic careers and will be in a position to identify the additional benefits of PFF to the department and to the institution. They will become a growing force in forging broader faculty and institutional support for better faculty preparation programs.

The social science and humanities disciplines have provided numerous venues for disseminating information about the benefits of PFF to their disciplines and to individual doctoral programs within the disciplines. They have included sessions at society meetings highlighting this fourth phase of PFF, and all of the societies have included sessions at future meetings and planned articles for future issues of society journals and newsletters. These societies understand that real change in the culture of preparation of future faculty requires a continued and sustained effort to promote the goals of PFF programs. Furthermore, the societies are committed to these goals and to the long-term efforts and activities that are necessary to achieve them. The connections among humanities and social science disciplines should encourage additional societies to mirror these efforts, resulting in broader support across the disciplines.

The PFF sponsoring associations, CGS and AAC&U, both will continue to promote the goals of PFF among leaders of graduate and undergraduate education and hiring institutions. These two organizations can convene gatherings and disseminate information to members and thereby help to maintain the interactive connections among PFF programs and between programs and disciplinary societies. Several other educational associations also have embraced many of the goals of PFF. These associations will help solidify and broaden support for PFF programs among other stakeholders of doctoral education, especially academic administrators.

## Securing broader support for PFF

Faculty and administrative support are necessary for the success of future faculty preparation programs because all faculty work occurs within an environment that is determined by the mission and, increasingly, the strategic plan of the institution. Administrative officials endorse faculty aspirations for graduate programs as institutional priorities. The support of academic and institutional administrators is necessary to institutionalize PFF as an integral part of the academic culture. Educational associations can help build collective support for these programs not only among faculty, but also among presidents, provosts, and other leaders who influence higher educational policies.

Securing university and external support for PFF programs will require that departments:

▲ Learn new strategies for "marketing" PFF programs that demonstrate demand from students and employers as well as benefits to students, the institution, and various constituents;

▲ Increase the visibility of departmental PFF programs, both internally and among external groups such as hiring institutions, state agencies, and alumni;

▲ Relate PFF programs to institutional and departmental strategic plans;

▲ Advocate policies that reward faculty for PFF participation, including mentoring in areas other than research; and

▲ Document the resources needed to support faculty preparation programs.

# A Confluence of Forces for Change

A confluence of forces has developed in recent years for improving the preparation of future faculty. These forces are the result of the efforts of the disciplinary societies and departmental clusters that participated in this fourth phase of PFF, several initiatives in graduate and undergraduate education, and societal factors. To envision the future of faculty preparation programs, the experience of the PFF program must be considered along with these forces and the initiatives that share many overlapping and intersecting goals, strategies, and even players. It is quite likely that future faculty preparation programs will result from successfully linking PFF to other change initiatives and incorporating new information and ways of thinking about both undergraduate and graduate education.

## Initiatives in doctoral education

Several recent studies of doctoral education have reflected a consensus among educational, business, and government leaders. These studies affirm research as the core requirement for the Ph.D. degree, but they suggest that additional requirements, including skills development, experiential learning, and career preparation are also important (Committee on Science, Engineering, and Public Policy 1995). The recommendations do not constitute a major restructuring of doctoral education, but they do represent a programmatic or cultural change that graduate faculty must embrace in order to change the academic culture. Several national initiatives have been launched to respond to the perceived need to effect changes in doctoral education (see Sidebar).

All of these efforts are compatible with the vision of PFF, and many have been stimulated to some extent by PFF. They reinforce each other and

## Initiatives to Improve Doctoral Education

The Carnegie Initiative on the Doctorate, of the Carnegie Foundation for the Advancement of Teaching, is studying changes in doctoral programs at selected departments in six fields of study and will disseminate its findings in order to foster the development of "stewards of the discipline." www.carnegiefoundation.org/CID/docs/CID_Overview.pdf

The Compact for Faculty Diversity is a collaboration of three regional higher education compacts and states  and graduate institutions in each region to promote the preparation of minority students for faculty positions. www.aypf.org/rmaa/pdfs/Compact.pdf

The Forum on Faculty Roles and Rewards of the American Association for Higher Education compiles information on the changing roles of faculty, broadening definitions of scholarship, academic careers, and transitions. www.boerner.net/conferences/conf_AAHE-FFRR.html

Preparing Future Professionals programs prepare graduate students for non-academic positions. Like PFF, PFP allows students to explore opportunities in organizations where they might work. www.utexas.edu/ogs/outreach/rc/communicator.html

Re-envisioning the Ph.D. is a University of Washington project that gathers information on perceptions, critiques, initiatives on graduate education, employer expectations, and other issues. A major national conference resulted in recommendations for various key constituents to improve the degree. www.grad.washington.edu/envision/

The Responsive PhD project of the Woodrow Wilson National Fellowship Foundation explores ways for the degree to be more responsive to social and academic change. These include new paradigms (e.g., interdisciplinarity), new practices (e.g., preparation for teaching), and new people (e.g., more diverse populations). www.woodrow.org/responsivephd/initiative.html

collectively point toward a change in the "culture of preparation" of future faculty.

Based on a growing body of research, these several initiatives hold promise to develop more welcoming, more informative, and more supportive pathways for graduate students to become faculty members, pathways that would incorporate many of the concepts and values of PFF.

## Initiatives in undergraduate education

Undergraduate education is changing in research universities that anchor the clusters as well as in their PFF partner institutions. The PFF students who have been involved at partner institutions in revising general education requirements, infusing diversity into the curriculum, and establishing writing programs across the curriculum, for example, have learned a great deal about both education and faculty politics. These are new elements in doctoral education, and integrating them into Ph.D. programs will require program planners and administrators to learn about them as well. Several organizations that currently sponsor initiatives in undergraduate education can supply information that will be useful both to directors of future faculty preparation programs and to students preparing for faculty careers (see Sidebar).

Regional accrediting bodies now require colleges and universities to assess student learning and to demonstrate educational effectiveness as a condition of accreditation. To maintain accreditation, institutions must establish clear learning goals, design curricula to help students achieve those goals, and demonstrate that goals are met. The regional and specialized accreditation agencies represent additional useful resources to help faculty, students, and institutions learn about and meet the new standards.

## Undergraduate education initiatives sponsored by various organizations

**Assessment:** Assessment Forum of the American Association for Higher Education; www.aahe.org/assessment

**Diversity:** Association of American Colleges and Universities
See *Diversity Digest* newsletter, www.diversityweb.org

**Freshman and senior year programs:** National Resource Center for the First-Year Experience and Students in Transition, University of South Carolina; www.fye.sc.edu/fye

**Interdisciplinary studies:** Association for Integrative Studies; www.muc.muohio.edu/~ais/index.htmlx

**Learning communities:** Washington Center for Improving Undergraduate Education, Evergreen State University; www.washcntr@evergreen.edu

**Writing across the curriculum:** Council of Writing Program Administrators; www.english.ilstu.edu/Hesse/wpawelcome.htm

An overview of these initiatives and trends can be obtained from two Washington, DC educational associations that can serve as resources for faculty preparation programs:

▲ **The American Association for Higher Education,** www.aahe.org; AAHE is an individual membership organization that sponsors publications, an annual national conference, topical conferences, funded projects, and an academy for academic change.

▲ **The Association of American Colleges and Universities,** www.aacu.org; AAC&U is an institutional membership organization that sponsors publications, an annual meeting, a series of working conferences, and demonstration projects on important developments in undergraduate education.

## Trends in public policy and funding

The burden for promoting doctoral programs that are more responsive to student and societal needs does not rest entirely upon faculty, disciplinary societies, and academic organizations such as CGS and AAC&U. There also are trends in public policy and in education funding that should enhance these individual and group efforts.

States are requiring that universities play a larger role in economic and social development and in the improvement of public education. These expectations support the primary PFF goals of improving undergraduate education, better preparing students for academic careers, and responding to the needs of hiring institutions.

Alumni and friends of universities provide an important source of private funding for universities, as reflected in the number and increasing goals of capital campaigns reported regularly in the *Chronicle of Higher Education.* The experience of the University of Iowa in its current campaign is typical of that reported by many institutions: there is high interest among donors in programs that directly support student needs and, especially, career preparation. Including graduate education among the university's priorities for fundraising is a relatively recent addition at Iowa and at most institutions. A compelling argument to persons able to contribute private funds is that graduates of the future are going to need substantial graduate education to accomplish what past graduates have accomplished with an undergraduate, or perhaps some graduate education. Private donors are also interested in programs that respond to the needs of employers and that include among their goals the improvement of education.

Federal funds account for a significant fraction of the support for graduate education, primarily through research and education grant programs.

Programs such as NSF's Integrated Graduate Education and Research Traineeship (IGERT) indicate the increasing importance of a training grant model that supports students in highly structured graduate programs. Training grants require that the program establish transparent processes for moving students toward clear educational and research goals by faculty with related or complementary expertise and research-focused interests. The training grant model of public support for graduate education reinforces the collaborative nature of PFF programs, as well as many of the PFF concepts and components.

## Demographic factors

The demographic composition of the US population poses challenges for programs that prepare future faculty in the social sciences and humanities. African Americans, Hispanics, American Indians, and persons with disabilities are underrepresented in these disciplines. For example, of the 5,058 social science doctoral degrees awarded to US citizens and permanent residents in 2001, only 34 were earned by American Indians, 197 by Asian Americans, 243 by Hispanic Americans, and 299 by African Americans (Hoffer, *et al*, 2002). These groups are also severely underrepresented among full-time postsecondary faculty in the social and behavioral sciences at four-year institutions; in 1999, 5.5 percent were African Americans, 4.8 percent were Asian Americans, 2.6 percent were Hispanic Americans, and 1.0 percent were American Indian or Alaskan Natives (National Science Foundation 2002, Appendix Table 2-6.)

These demographics pose several challenges to faculty preparation programs:

▲ **To recruit and graduate more Ph.D.s from underrepresented groups, thereby developing a cohort of diverse, well-trained faculty.** An important strategy already discussed is to create linkages and connections to other national programs that seek to increase the number of minority doctoral graduates.

*Although the percentage of minorities making up the nation's population and entering our colleges and universities as undergraduates is on the rise, professors standing at the front of the class remain largely white and, in some disciplines, predominately male. In English, as one example, the number of African American Ph.D. graduates seems frozen at about 3.5%, no greater than 30 years ago. The number rises slightly in the social sciences . . . . The lack of role models for students often means that lack of diversity perpetuates itself, and ultimately renders learning provincial, as new studies on the intellectual benefits of diversity have shown. Student retention at earlier stages of education is of course a crucial part of the solution, but doctoral programs must do their part to develop new recruitment and retention strategies to ensure role models for future students, and a cosmopolitan vibrancy for their disciplines.*

The Woodrow Wilson National Fellowship Foundation
www.woodrow.org/responsivephd/agenda.html

▲ **To more effectively recruit faculty from underrepresented groups.**
Faculty search committees need assistance in their efforts to identify
and recruit minority candidates. Toward this end, the PFF program
joined other groups in supporting the preparation of a guidebook for
faculty search committees, *Diversifying the Faculty* (Turner 2002). It
discusses steps to take before the search begins, during the search
process, and after the search, including ways to support the person
hired.

▲ **To equip future faculty to serve the needs of diverse student
groups.** Faculty preparation programs should help future faculty
learn approaches to education that are welcoming to all students
(Chism and Pruitt 1995). This requires that graduate students be
exposed to a broad range of strategies to address diversity issues,
from adopting interpersonal and pedagogical approaches to creating
inclusive curricula and classrooms that engage students from diverse
backgrounds, to acquiring experience at colleges and universities
with diverse student bodies. The goal is for doctoral graduates to be
exposed to curriculum issues and to develop teaching skills that will
make them more effective educators and mentors to students of all
backgrounds.

## Professional education expectations

A fundamental premise of professional education is that one prepares for a
profession by experiencing the variety of settings in which it is practiced.
Preparation for most professions involves an assortment of internships, resi-
dencies, and fieldwork that is seldom part of preparation for the professoriate.

For example, some law students work in legal clinics, and others work as interns in law firms or with judges, practicing the work of the profession for which they are preparing. While still studying toward their degrees, seminarians work in parishes and preach. These practices are more than simply experiential education, as valuable as that may be. A new doctor must know a great deal about anatomy and pharmaceuticals but must also have experience treating patients. Similarly, it is not sufficient for faculty to know only the content of their fields; they also must be effective teachers and advisors, be able to relate to students as learners, and participate in institutional governance. The cluster of diverse PFF institutions provides professional and practical experiences for prospective faculty.

The significant body of research on the academic profession provides another resource for faculty preparation. For example, this literature includes research and scholarship on the effectiveness of: different approaches to teaching (McKeachie 1999; Menges, Weimer, and Associates 1996); student learning (Bransford, Brown, and Cocking 1999; Chickering and Gamson 1987); the curriculum (Gaff and Ratcliff 1997); assessment of student performance (López 1999); and the impact of college on students (Astin 1993; Pascarella and Terenzini 1991). Similarly, there is a scholarly literature about the operation of colleges and universities and about professional concepts such as academic freedom, shared governance, and peer review, which students seldom encounter in graduate school, but which is important to their preparation and practice as professionals.

Doctoral education should be rich in opportunities for professional development, assuredly in the conduct of research, but also in other ways that are important to the future careers of doctoral students.

# Strategies for increasing the impact of PFF

## Expand the range of faculty preparation programs

The PFF program created opportunities for only a small number of doctoral students across the disciplines. Assessments and personal testimony indicate that these programs are useful to students, faculty, departments, and disciplines. In addition to these preliminary indicators, the placement records and career trajectories of PFF faculty alumni will provide additional evidence relating to the impact of PFF.

The four phases of the PFF program were funded by grants from several agencies and foundations. Similar professional development programs for graduate students have been established at several other universities, often without such external funding. For example, Syracuse University and Emory University both established professional development programs similar to PFF before PFF was initiated. Claremont Graduate University, University of Michigan, University of Missouri, Vanderbilt University, and Virginia Commonwealth University have all created university-wide programs similar to PFF in the past few years. Departmental programs were established in communication at Eastern Michigan University and in criminology at Indiana University of Pennsylvania. Typically, leaders at these institutions interacted with PFF leaders and consulted with other institutions, borrowing from the extensive programmatic resources available.

In planning future faculty preparation programs, the experiences and lessons of both the PFF programs and these related but independent programs constitute rich resources.

## Stimulate a market demand for professionally prepared faculty

Enhancing the preparation of new social science and humanities faculty members is a complex undertaking that requires strategic partnerships and alliances of college and university faculty, central administrators, governing bodies, and other policy makers. An important incentive for establishing such alliances is the demand of the hiring community for the type of preparation that is offered by PFF programs. For example, in a statement that specifies the qualities they seek in new faculty, the Commonwealth Colleges of Pennsylvania, a consortium of liberal arts colleges, listed the very qualities PFF programs seek to develop—strengths in teaching, research, and service (Commonwealth Partnership, 1996). At all types of hiring institutions—including research universities—central administrators, members of governing boards, and policy makers can insist that faculty hires be broadly prepared and demonstrate these strengths.

Groups of institutions organized around distinctive missions can take similar initiatives. Orlando Taylor, Dean of the Graduate School at Howard University, organized summit meetings for presidents of historically black colleges and universities (HBCUs) that led to a call for prospective faculty to better understand the missions of their institutions and to look forward to working there. Another goal of these meetings was to encourage other HBCUs to become PFF anchor and partner institutions.

Faculty search committees can set higher expectations and expect more documentation about professional accomplishment from candidates. A recent review of research identifies several common expectations of colleges and universities for new faculty (Adams 2002): effective teaching that engages students and supports learning; a program of research suited to the circumstances and resources of the institution; and active involvement in the academic life of the campus, including shared governance. Having been involved in the Duke University cluster as a partner faculty mentor, Kathrynn Adams specifically recommends that PFF elements be included more prominently in doctoral programs. She also cites evidence that doctoral students need more assistance with job searches and greater awareness of career options in a variety of colleges and universities.

These kinds of actions can stimulate a demand for more effectively prepared new faculty. If hiring institutions put a premium on such preparation, graduate departments are more likely to be persuaded to provide this experience for their doctoral students. It would be refreshing to see more advertisements for faculty like the one issued by the department of psychology at Occidental College in November 2001, which states explicitly, "PFF experience preferred."

## Foster professional development as a component of financial aid programs

Teaching assistantships and fellowships are the typical forms of financial support for social science and humanities graduate students. The policies and requirements of agencies that provide the funding can substantially influence university or departmental policies and practices. Thus, funding agencies could be excellent prospective partners for faculty preparation programs if they weighed professional development components of graduate programs as positive factors in decisions to award funds.

Teaching assistantships often are seen as a way to cover instructional obligations rather than as opportunities for graduate students to grow as teachers and scholars (Nyquist, *et al.* 2001). Although excellent teaching assistant development programs do exist (Marincovich, Prostco, and Stout 1998), they do not reach all graduate students who could benefit from them, and often they focus on classroom management rather than on the intellectual challenges of teaching a range of students or designing undergraduate curricula. As directors of teaching assistant development programs know, graduate students improve their teaching skills and expand their teaching repertoire when they are introduced to the rich literature on teaching and learning. They begin to analyze and solve instructional problems, understand how teaching their discipline relates to relevant social needs and problems, and devise effective ways to assess learning.

Fellowships are highly valued funding mechanisms because they free students from any commitments to either research or teaching. But fellowship holders with an interest in an academic career have asked to participate in PFF programs. They recognize that PFF courses, workshops, seminars, and internships are important in preparing and being competitive for faculty positions. As Barbara Lovitts (2001) suggests, teaching and research assistantships may help integrate students into the social fabric of their graduate programs, enhance their education, and aid them in completing their degree.

Syracuse University created a Future Professoriate Project (FPP) that offered participants opportunities to teach, provided "teaching mentors," encouraged students to develop a "teaching portfolio," and awarded a Certificate in College Teaching. University fellowship recipients subsequently requested the same opportunities, and the university developed a modified FPP program for them.

In order to provide professional development opportunities, the Graduate School at Howard University requires all students funded by educational grants to participate in PFF.

These examples illustrate that requiring graduate students with fellowships to be involved in a professional development program has inherent value that complements the benefits of developing research competencies and completing studies in a timely manner.

## Envisioning the Future of Doctoral Education

The project that has been the subject of this volume has documented not just the feasibility but also the desirability of incorporating PFF programs in the social sciences and humanities. It replicates the previous project that documented the desirability of making PFF a part of graduate preparation for faculty in the natural sciences and mathematics. Abundant experience and evidence has been accumulated by thousands of individuals in hundreds of institutions to document that PFF works.

Given the preponderance of this experience and evidence, one wonders: Why isn't everyone involved in the graduate preparation of future faculty industriously establishing such programs for their students? The first chapter discussed the phenomenon of inertia in colleges and universities, and that seems to be a major reason why PFF remains the exception rather than the rule. Despite the rapid growth and expansion of PFF programs, they still serve a relatively small number of those who could benefit from them.

Another reason is that many faculty members who are guardians of doctoral education have not learned about the high expectations that colleges and universities are placing on new faculty, the difficulties their graduate students face in securing suitable academic positions, the benefits that PFF confers, and the relatively low investment that PFF programs require. This suggests that next steps for PFF include a more aggressive campaign to educate faculty members, students, and administrators responsible for doctoral education of the need for PFF. The disciplinary societies, educational associations, and special projects supporting doctoral education should play proactive roles in educating their colleagues about the power of PFF.

Precisely because these challenges persist, the need to aggressively promote PFF exists. Fortunately, PFF continues to gain momentum. More leaders are attracted to the PFF vision, new PFF programs are being established, and existing ones are being expanded. Indeed, given the growth of research into doctoral education and the rise of related projects to improve education at all levels, PFF is helping to lead the reform of doctoral education.

More research into the outcomes of PFF programs is needed. But with over 4,000 doctoral students having been involved in PFF programs as "core participants," along with over 1,000 faculty members, and scores of program directors and administrators, a great deal of experience and evidence has been accumulated. It is time to conclude that PFF is a more effective education for doctoral students preparing for a faculty career than the traditional approach that focuses almost entirely on preparing for a research career. Leaders of related initiatives to improve doctoral education would be encouraged to build on the success of PFF programs and to draw on the resources that have been accumulated to enhance their own impact.

What would the culture of doctoral education look like if there were more widespread reform? Leaders of PFF and the disciplinary societies envision a future in which doctoral education would be a collective responsibility. It would be owned by the program faculty, assuredly, but they would be in close consultation with those who employ Ph.D. graduates, both within and beyond the academy. The core requirement of doctoral programs would continue to be the mastery of knowledge and the ability to perform research that expands the boundaries of the discipline. Assimilation of knowledge and acquisition of skills would occur, however, less within the narrow focus of a specialization than within a broader context of the discipline and with greater interaction with peers and those from other disciplines—better reflecting the interdisciplinary trends in undergraduate liberal education as well as the nature of many professional workplaces.

Students would be socialized into their graduate program and the discipline very early. They would learn about subjects that are important to modern intellectual work but seldom a standard feature of graduate programs, such as ethics and intellectual property issues. They would also develop skills that are critical to teaching and research in the academy as well as other professions, such as communicating with peers and audiences of varied backgrounds. Information on the range of career opportunities available to graduates would be provided to prospective students, and career advising and planning assistance would be available to students throughout their graduate programs. As a result, students would be prepared to make informed decisions on program selection and options within them that fit their specific career objectives.

A common option or requirement would be an internship in a work environment representative of what graduates may experience in their careers, just as PFF students work with a teaching mentor. Advanced students would serve as resources to the program and as peer mentors to beginning students. Adjunct appointments of alumni and other professional from non-academic work environments would become more common, and these adjuncts would be readily available to students for mentoring both in research and in other aspects of professional life. Preparing to search for a position and establishing a career would be components of the program for all students, regardless of career choice. Continuing education would become a hallmark of programs, with graduates offering instruction that assist in career advancement and ensuring currency in the discipline. In return, the alumni would support and often be actively involved in the graduate program.

Embedded within this larger vision of doctoral education are faculty preparation programs. Courses in these programs would examine pace-setting educational changes in both disciplines and in the general education programs for which the majority of humanities and social science faculty will eventually bear responsibility. They will explore the shift from "teaching" to "learning" and the implications of this shift for faculty roles. Active participants in such initiatives would include the faculty of a program's partnering institutions, which hire many new Ph.D.s. PFF alumni who become faculty at partner institutions would re-enter the program as partner faculty and offer learning opportunities and mentoring to future cohorts of doctoral students, giving back benefits they gained to yet another generation of faculty. In this way, faculty preparation programs would sustain the excellence and flexibility of the academic enterprise to meet the changing needs of the society it serves.

# Appendix I

# Disciplinary Societies' Strategies to Sustain PFF Programs

Each disciplinary society participating in this project plans to build on their model cluster programs as they continue advocating for PFF in their discipline and encouraging the spread of such programs. They view PFF within a "larger vision of the profession" and among society programs that add value for even modest investment of resources. Societies thus will feature PFF—formally and prominently—in their national and regional meetings, websites and electronic discussion groups. They also will continue to disseminate publications and information about PFF and educate their members about the rationale and benefits of PFF programs and strategies for establishing them. Plans of each society for promoting faculty preparation programs are enumerated below.

**The American Historical Association (AHA)** has started "friends of PFF," a professional network of faculty involved in PFF and others interested in it, to promote discussion and to assist others in starting programs. An AHA survey of educational programs of departments included questions relating to professional development of graduate students. The results will be widely discussed by historians in all kinds of institutions, providing ample opportunity to consider PFF and other improvements in history graduate education.

The American Psychological Association (APA), through its Office of Graduate Education and Training in its Education Directorate, has endorsed PFF. APA will seek ways to sustain existing PFF programs and to significantly increase their number, especially in those departments with strong records of recruiting and graduating minority students. They plan to integrate PFF programs into the disciplinary activities that focus on the scholarship of teaching and learning, with an emphasis on the engaged scholar with service to the community. A faculty workshop on starting a psychology department PFF program will be developed, field tested, and highlighted at various APA meetings.

The American Political Science Association (APSA) is concerned that prospective graduate students know little about the graduate programs to which they apply and that faculty candidates have little knowledge of departmental environments and the expectations for new faculty. To address these concerns, the APSA Committee on Education and Professional Development has developed a Rostering Program and a Registration Program. These programs are expected to make the programs of the department more transparent to prospective students and faculty.

Both the Rostering and the Registration programs pose questions to departments concerning their expectations for the preparation of new faculty and the support for teaching, research, and service. In addition, the Rostering Program includes questions on professional training components of the doctoral programs. Departments that elect to participate in the Rostering program agree to make their answers available to students applying to their program. The Registration program includes additional questions relating to professional development opportunities for newly appointed faculty. Faculty candidates are encouraged to refer to both the Rostering and Registering information during the application process and when considering a job offer. Information about these programs and lists of signatory and participating departments are available at the following websites: <www.apsanet.org/about/chairs/rostering.cfm> (Rostering Program) and <www.apsanet.org/about/chairs/registration.cfm> (Registration Program).

The American Sociological Associations (ASA) has organized "friends of PFF" that includes both departments with phase four funding and those not selected for funding, as well as students and faculty from PFF phases one and two. The organization promotes communication among participants from all four phases of the PFF program. The Society's *Guide to Graduate Departments in Sociology* (2002) lists departmental programs for preparing graduates for faculty positions as an effective way to encourage students to consider the value of such programs as PFF in selecting a graduate program.

ASA meetings include graduate program poster sessions, and prospective students increasingly ask whether departments have a PFF program. Such expressions of interest by prospective students encourage graduate programs to offer better faculty preparation.

The National Communication Association (NCA) authorized small matching grants to departments to develop model faculty preparation programs as early as 1996, before the funding for the fourth phase of PFF was available. The goal was to use small seed grants to leverage inter-institutional partnerships within the discipline to support better preparation of doctoral students for a variety of faculty positions. With the support of its Committee on Doctoral Education, NCA intends to continue promoting PFF. Successive chairs of this committee have been national leaders of PFF and of strategies to effectively incorporate PFF within the graduate education programs of the discipline.

The executive director of NCA and the chair of its PFF leadership team have made site visits to all four of its clusters to meet with academic deans and provosts, and to help solidify the cluster as a model of best practice. These visits have secured institutional commitment of continued funding of the current PFF programs. The four NCA clusters intend to actively encourage the establishment of additional clusters and, once established, to serve in an advisory role to the new programs. With resources from NCA, these clusters will promote dialogue about PFF within their geographical regions.

**The National Council of Teachers of English (NCTE)** urges visitors to its website to join the "Friends of PFF listserv." The Council intends to further develop PFF within each of its four constituent higher education groups—the Conference on Composition and Communication, the College Section, the Conference on English Education, and the Two-Year College English Association. For example, the Two-Year College English Association is developing guidelines for the preparation of community college English teachers, and all the NCTE higher education groups will advocate the inclusion of PFF concepts in all curricular areas of graduate English programs.

# Appendix II

# Faculty Leaders and Partner Institutions in PFF Phase Four

## American Historial Association

Noralee Frankel, Assistant Director, Women, Minorities, and Teaching, American Historical Association, 400 A Street SE, Washington DC 20003, Ph: (202) 544-2422, Fax (202) 544-8307, Email: nfrankel@theaha.org

## Arizona State University

Noel J. Stowe, Chair and Professor, Department of History, Arizona State University, History Department, P.O. Box 872501, Tempe, AZ 85287-2501, Ph: (480) 965-5779, Fax: (480) 965-0310, Email: noel.stowe@asu.edu

Partner Institutions: Arizona State University-East, Arizona State University-West, Chandler Gilbert Community College, Grand Canyon University, Phoenix College, Scottsdale Community College

## Boston College

Robin Fleming, Director of Graduate Studies, Professor of History, Boston College, Department of History, McGuinn Hall Room 221, Chestnut Hill, MA 02167, Ph: (617) 552-8484, Fax: (617) 552-3700, Email: fleminra@monet.bc.edu

Partner Institutions: Emmanuel College, Framingham State College, Simmons College

## Florida State University

Jonathan Grant, Professor, Florida State University, History Department, Tallahassee, FL, 32306-2200, Ph: (850) 644-5888, Fax: (850) 644-6402, Email: jgrant@mailer.fsu.edu

Partner Institutions: Bainbridge College, Florida A&M University, Rollins College, Tallahassee Community College, Thomas College, Valdosta State University

## Howard University

Jeanne Maddox Toungara, Assistant Professor, Howard University, Department of History, Douglas Hall, 2441 6th Street, NW, Washington, DC 20059, Ph: (202) 806-6800, Fax: (202) 806-4471, Email: jtoungara@howard.edu

Partner Institutions: Bowie State University, The Catholic University of America, Howard Community College, Marymount University

# American Political Science Association

Sheilah Mann, Director, Education and Professional Dev., American Political Science Association, 1527 New Hampshire Avenue NW, Washington DC 20036, Ph: (202) 483-2512, Fax (202) 483-2657, Email: smann@apsanet.org

## Howard University

Alvin Thornton, Associate Dean, Political Science, Howard University, Office of the Provost, Douglas Hall, Washington, DC 20059, Ph: (202) 806-6720, Fax: (202) 265-3527, Email: athornton@fac.howard.edu

Partner Institutions: Bowie State University, The Catholic University of America, Howard Community College, Marymount University, Prince George's Community College

## Indiana University

Norman Furniss, Professor of Political Science, Indiana University,
  Woodburn Hall 210, 1100 E 7th Street, Bloomington, IN 47405-7110,
  Ph: (812) 855-9100, Fax: (812) 855-2027, Email: furniss@indiana.edu

Partner Institutions: DePauw University, Indiana University-Purdue University
  Fort Wayne, Indiana University-Purdue University Indianapolis, Wabash
  College

## University of Colorado at Boulder

Susan Clarke, Graduate Director, Professor, University of Colorado at Boulder,
  Department of Political Science, Campus Box 333, Boulder, CO 80309-
  0330, Ph: (303) 492-2953, Fax: (303) 492-0978,
  Email: susan.clarke@colorado.edu

Partner Institutions: Metro State University, San José State University,
  Stanford University, University of Colorado-Denver, United States Air
  Force Academy

## University of Illinois at Chicago

Dick Simpson, Professor, University of Illinois at Chicago, Department of
  Political Science, (M/C 276), 1007 West Harrison Street, Chicago, IL
  60607-7137, Ph: (312) 413-3780, Fax: (312) 413-0440,
  Email: simpson@uic.edu

Partner Institutions: Chicago State University, City Colleges of Chicago
  (Richard J. Daley College and Wilbur Wright College), Elmhurst College,
  Illinois Wesleyan University, Joliet Junior College, Roosevelt University,
  University of Illinois-Springfield, Western Illinois University, William
  Rainey Harper College

## American Psychological Association

Paul Nelson, Deputy Executive Director, Education Directorate, American
    Psychological Association, 750 First Street NE, Washington DC 20002-
    4242, Ph: (202) 374-2721, Fax (202) 336-5500, Email: PNelson@apa.org

## Miami University

Cecilia Shore, Associate Professor, Miami University, Department of
    Psychology, Benton Hall, Oxford, OH 45056, Ph: (513) 529-2401,
    Fax: (513) 529-2420, Email: shorec@muohio.edu
Partner Institutions: College of Mount Saint Joseph, Earlham College,
    Northern Kentucky University, Miami University-Hamilton, Miami
    University-Middletown

## University of Colorado at Boulder

Irene Blair, Assistant Professor, University of Colorado at Boulder,
    Department of Psychology, Campus Box 345, Muenzinger D244,
    Boulder, CO 80309-0345, Ph: (303) 492-4563, Fax: (303) 492-2967,
    Email: irene.blair@colorado.edu
Partner Institutions: Colorado College, Connecticut College, Yale University

## University of Georgia

Rosemary Phelps, Associate Professor, University of Georgia, Department of
    Counseling and Human Development Services, College of Education,
    402 Aderhold Hall, Athens, GA 30602-7142, Ph: (706) 542-4221,
    Fax: (706) 542-4130, Email: rphelps@coe.uga.edu
Partner Institutions: Kennesaw State University, Morehouse College,
    Morehouse School of Medicine, North Georgia College and State
    University

## University of New Hampshire

Victor Benassi, Associate Vice President for Academic Affairs, University of
New Hampshire, Academic Affairs, Thompson Hall, P.O. Box 645020,
Durham, NH 03824

Ph: (603) 862-3290, Fax: (603) 862-4741, Email: vab@cisunix.unh.edu

Partner Institutions: Dartmouth College, Howard University, Keene State
College, New Hampshire Community Technical College, St. Anselm
College, University of New Hampshire-Manchester

# American Sociological Association

Carla Howery, Deputy Executive Officer, American Sociological Association,
1307 New York Avenue NW—Suite 700, Washington DC 20005, Ph:
(202) 383-9005, Fax: (202) 638-0882, Email: howery@asanet.org

## Indiana University

Bernice Pescosolido, Chancellors' Professor of Sociology, Indiana University,
Department of Sociology, 744 Ballantine Hall, Bloomington, IN 47405,
Ph: (812) 855-3841, Fax: (812) 856-5713, Email: pescosol@indiana.edu

Partner Institutions: Butler University, DePauw University, Marian College,
Indiana University-Columbus, Indiana University-Purdue University
Indianapolis, Indiana University-South Bend, Morehouse College

## North Carolina State University

Barbara Risman, Director of Graduate Programs, Professor, North Carolina
    State University, Department of Sociology and Anthropology,
    Campus Box 8107, Raleigh, NC 27695-8107, Ph: (919) 515-9013,
    Fax: (919) 513-1120, Email: barbara_risman@ncsu.edu

Partner Institutions: College of Charleston, Elon University, North Carolina
    Central University, University of North Carolina-Greensboro, University
    of North Carolina-Wilmington

## Texas A&M University

Harland Prechel, Associate Professor, Texas A&M University,
    Department of Sociology, College Station, TX 77843-4351,
    Ph: (409) 845-6424, Fax: (409) 862-4057, Email: h-prechel@tamu.edu

Partner Institutions: Blinn College, Our Lady of the Lake University, Prairie
    View A&M University, Sam Houston State University, Texas A&M
    International University, Texas Southern University, University of Texas
    at Pan American

## University of Nebraska

Helen Moore, Editor, Teaching Sociology, Professor, University of Nebraska,
    Department of Sociology, 711 Oldfather Hall, Lincoln, NE 68588-0324,
    Ph: (402) 472-6081, Fax: (402) 472-6070, Email: hmoore1@unl.edu

Partner Institutions: Alcorn State University, Grambling State University, Little
    Priest Tribal College, New Mexico Highlands University

# National Communication Association

Sherry Morreale, Associate Director, National Communication Association, 1765 N Street NW, Washington DC 20036, Ph: (202) 464-4622, Fax (202) 464-4600, Email: smorreale@natcom.org

## Howard University

Melbourne Cummings, Department Chair, Professor, Howard University, School of Communications, 525 Bryant Street, NW, Washington, DC 20059, Ph: (202) 806-6711, Fax: (202) 387-3656, Email: mcummings@howard.edu

Partner Institutions: Bowie State University, The Catholic University of America, George Mason University, Prince George's Community College

## Indiana University

Patricia Hayes Andrews, Professor, Department of Communication and Culture, 809 East 7th Street, Bloomington, IN 47405-3999, Ph: (812) 855-4379, Fax: (812) 339-2735, Email: andrewsp@indiana.edu

Partner Institutions: Arizona State University-West, Butler University, Indiana University-Purdue University Fort Wayne, Indiana University-Purdue University Indianapolis, Manchester College, Texas A&M Kingsville, University of Indianapolis

## University of Kentucky

Roy Moore, Associate Dean for Graduate Studies, Professor of Journalism, University of Kentucky, College of Communications and Information Studies, Office of the Dean, Grehan Building, Lexington, KY 40506-0042, Ph: (606) 257-7805, Fax: (606) 323-9879,

Email: moore@pop.uky.edu

Partner Institutions: Asbury College, Centre College, Coventry University (UK), Eastern Kentucky University, Georgetown College, Kentucky State University, Lexington Community College, Murray State University, Transylvania University, University for Peace (Costa Rica)

## University of New Mexico

Janet Cramer, Coordinator, Preparing Future Faculty, University of New Mexico, Department of Communication and Journalism, Bldg. 115, Room 235 West, Albuquerque, NM 87131-1171, Ph: (505) 277-0095, Fax: (505) 277-4206, Email: jcramer@unm.edu

Partner Institutions: Albuquerque Technical-Vocational Institute, Armand Hammer United World College, New Mexico State University, St. John's College, Southwestern Indian Polytechnic Institute, University of New Mexico-Gallup, University of New Mexico-Los Alamos, University of New Mexico-Valencia

# National Council of Teachers of English

Paul Bodmer, Associate Executive Director, National Council of Teachers of English, 1111 West Kenyon Road, Urbana, IL 61801-1094, Ph: 1-800-369-6283, Fax: (217) 328-9645, Email: PBodmer@ncte.org

## Howard University

John Reilly, Graduate Program Director in English, Howard University, Alain Locke Hall, Room 248, Washington, DC 20059, Ph: (202) 806-7453, Fax: (202) 806-6708, Email: jreilly@howard.edu

Partner Institutions: The Catholic University of America, Howard Community College, Marymount University

## Michigan Technological University

Bob Johnson, Chair, Department of Humanities, Michigan Technological University, 319B Walker Arts and Humanities Center, 1400 Townsend Drive, Houghton, MI 49931-1295, Ph: (906) 487-2540, Fax: (906) 487-3559, Email: rrjohnso@mtu.edu

Partner Institutions: Bay de Noc Community College, Finlandia University, Keweenaw Bay Ojibwa Community College, Northern Michigan University, Wayne State University

## University of Illinois at Chicago

Patricia Harkin, Associate Professor of English, University of Illinois at Chicago, 601 South Morgan Street, Chicago, IL 60607-7120, Ph: (312) 413-7400, Fax: (312) 413-1005, Email: Pharkin@uic.edu

Partner Institutions: Elmhurst College, North Central College, Purdue University-Calumet

## University of South Florida

Debra Jacobs, Director of Composition, University of South Florida, Department of English, 4202 E. Fowler Avenue, CPR 107, Tampa, FL 33620, Ph: (813) 974-9473, Fax: (813) 974-2270, Email: djacobs@chuma.cas.usf.edu

Partner Institutions: Hillsborough Community College, Polk Community College, St. Petersburg College, University of Tampa

## Washington State University

George Kennedy, Associate Professor and Program Coordinator, Washington State University, Department of English, P.O. Box 645020, Pullman, WA 99164-5020, Ph: (509) 335-2680/2581, Fax: (509) 335-2582, Email: gkennedy@mail.wsu.edu

Partner Institutions: Northwest Indian College, Yakima Valley Community College-Grandview Campus

# Appendix III

# University of Nebraska Mentoring Contract

**As a PFF Mentee participating in PFF, I agree to:**

▲ Attend a colloquium on conducting classroom research (August 20, 2000).

▲ Sign the mentoring agreement.

▲ Contact my mentor by September 30, 2000 to discuss preliminary plans for my capstone project.

▲ Consult with the faculty mentor to plan what will be taught in teaching opportunities and what will be the classroom research process.

▲ Develop an IRB proposal for evaluation of student outcomes from the capstone project (deadline for submission is November 15, 2000).

▲ When on the host campus, meet intensively with the faculty mentor to discuss the teaching and learning process and the faculty role.

▲ Work with my mentor to explore one service opportunity and two aspects of the faculty role while on the host campus.

▲ Meet with the mentor before and after each teaching opportunity to discuss lesson plans and teaching feedback.

▲ Discuss the co-authorship of a report/potential publication to identify potential mutual interests and determine appropriate authorship expectations.

▲ Draft a ten-page report on the capstone project and student learning outcomes to be presented at the UNL Preparing Future Faculty Conference in April 2001.

*PFF Mentoring Contract, Sociology Department, University of Nebraska, Lincoln University of Nebraska, Lincoln. Preparing Future Faculty Mentoring. (Alcorn State University, Grambling State University, New Mexico Highlands University, Tribally Controlled Community Colleges).*

As a Faculty mentor participating in PFF, I agree to:

▲ Read and consider the attached materials on mentoring.

▲ Complete a mentor questionnaire, and sign the mentoring agreement.

▲ Confer with the mentee on his/her proposed capstone project and collaborate on identifying appropriate teaching opportunities. Discuss whether co-authorship of a report/potential publication is of mutual interest and determine appropriate authorship expectations following ASA professional standards.

▲ Observe at least two of the capstone project sessions during the mentee's visit. Meet for an hour before each session to discuss the content and teaching techniques to be used and an hour after each session to provide constructive feedback and participate in the evaluation of a classroom research component.

▲ Work with my mentee to explore one service opportunity and two aspects of the faculty role while the mentee is on the host campus (see the attached list of potential options).

▲ Provide written feedback on the report of the capstone project (possible collaboration on a co-authored article).

▲ Attend the PFF Capstone Workshop in April 2001 to confer with other faculty members and PFF Fellows and hear Fellows' reports.

▲ Attend or designate an appropriate candidate to attend the 2001 Preparing Future Faculty National Conference in Colorado Springs, Colorado.

*(All expenses for travel to Lincoln, NE and Colorado Springs conferences are covered by a grant from the American Sociological Association.)*

# References

Adams, K.A. 2002. *What colleges and universities want in new faculty.* PreparingFuture Faculty Occasional Paper Number 7. Washington, DC: Association of American Colleges and Universities and Council of Graduate Schools.

American Council on Education. 2001. *Higher education and national affairs.* October 22, 3.

American Sociological Association. 2002. *Guide to graduate departments of sociology.* Washington, DC.

Angelo, T. & K. P. Cross. 1993. *Classroom assessment techniques: A handbook for college teachers,* (2nd ed.). San Francisco: Jossey-Bass.

Applegate, J.L. 2002. *Engaged graduate education: Seeing with new eyes.* Preparing Future Faculty Occasional Paper Number 9. Washington, DC: Association of American Colleges and Universities and Council of Graduate Schools.

Astin, A.A. 1993. *What matters in college.* San Francisco: Jossey-Bass.

Austin, A.E. 2002. Preparing the next generation of faculty: Graduate school as socialization to the academic career. *Journal of Higher Education,* 73:1, 94-122.

Bashara, C.G.N. 2002. The last word: The impact of Preparing Future Faculty initiatives on new and future faculty. *Liberal Education,* 88:3, 54-59.

Benassi, V. and P. Fernald. 1993. Preparing tomorrow's psychologists for careers in academe. *Teaching of Psychology,* 20, 149-155.

Berger, A., R. Kirshstein, and E. Rowe. 2001. U.S. Department of Education, National Center for Education Statistics (NCES). *Institutional Policies and Practices: Results from the 1999 National Study of Postsecondary Faculty, Institution Survey.* Table 2.1. Washington, DC.

Boyer, E. 1990. *Scholarship reconsidered: Priorities of the professoriate.* Baltimore: Carnegie Foundation.

Bransford, J.D., A.L. Brown, and R.R. Cocking, eds. 1999. *How people learn: Brain, mind, experience, and school.* Washington, DC: National Academy Press.

Chickering, A.W. and Z. Gamson. 1987. Seven principles for good practice in undergraduate education. *AAHE Bulletin.* Washington, DC: American Association for Higher Education.

Chism, N.Van N. and A.S. Pruitt. 1995. Promoting inclusiveness in college teaching. In W.A. Wright, ed. *Teaching improvement practices: successful strategies for higher education.* Bolton, MA: Anker Publishing Company, 325-345.

Clarke, S.E., P. Hutchings, S. Keeter, G. Reeher, Y. Alex-Assensoh, and F. Boyd. 2002. Transcript: Roundtable on the scholarship of teaching and learning in political science. *PS: Political Science and Politics.* June. Washington, DC: American Political Science Association.

Committee on Science, Engineering, and Public Policy (COSEPUP). 1995. *Reshaping the graduate education of scientists and engineers.* Washington, DC: National Academy Press.

Commonwealth Partnership. 1996. *What you should know: An open letter to new Ph.D.s.* Lancaster, PA: Franklin and Marshall College.

Cross, K. P. and M. H. Steadman.1996. *Classroom research: Implementing the scholarship of teaching.* San Francisco: Jossey-Bass.

DeNeef, A.L. 2002. *The Preparing Future Faculty program: What difference does it make?* Preparing Future Faculty Occasional Paper Number 8. Washington, DC: Association of American Colleges and Universities and Council of Graduate Schools.

Education Trust-West. 2002. *The high school diploma: Making it more than an empty promise.* Testimony by Russlynn Ali. Oakland.

Gaff, J.G. 2002. The disconnect: Graduate education and faculty realities: A review of recent research. *Liberal Education, "Changing Course: Preparing Faculty for the Future,"* 88: 3, 6-13.

Gaff, J.G. and J.L. Ratcliff. 1997. *Handbook of the undergraduate curriculum.* San Francisco: Jossey-Bass.

Golde, C.M. and T. M. Dore. 2001. *At cross purposes: What the experiences of today's graduate students reveal about doctoral education.* Philadelphia: The Pew Charitable Trusts.

Hecker, D.E. 2001. Occupational employment projection to 2010. *Monthly Labor Review*, 124: 11.

Hoffer, T., B. Dugoni, A. Sanderson, S. Sederstrom, R. Ghadialy, and P. Pocque. 2001.

*Doctorate recipients from United States universities: Summary report 2000.* Chicago: National Opinion Research Center. (Produced by NORC for NSF, NIH,USED,NEH, USDA, and NASA.) www.nsf.gov/sbe/srs/sendgr/start.htm

Hoffer, T.B., B. Dugoni, A. Sanderson, S. Sederstrom, V. Welch, I. Guzman-Barron, and S. Brown. 2002. *Doctorate recipients from United States universities: summary report 2001.* Table 26. Chicago: National Opinion Research Center. (Data from the Survey of Earned Doctorates, conducted for NSF, NIH, USED, NEH, USDA, and NASA by NORC).

Huber, M.T. and S.P. Morreale, eds. 2002. *Disciplinary styles in scholarship of teaching and learning: Exploring common ground.* Washington, DC: American Association of Higher Education and the Carnegie Foundation for the Advancement of Teaching.

Ingram L. and P. Brown. 1997. *Humanities doctorates in the United States: 1995 profile.* Washington, DC: National Academy Press.

LaPidus, J.B. 1995. Doctoral education and student career needs. In Pruitt, A.S. and P.D. Issac, eds. *Student services for the changing graduate student population,* New Directions for Student Services, Number 72. San Francisco: Jossey-Bass.

Lee, R. 2001. Justifying Preparing Future Faculty programs. *Liberal Education,* 87: 2, 46-51.

López, C. 1999. A decade of assessing student learning: What we have learned. What's Next? Presented at the 104th Annual Meeting of the North Central Association/Commission on Institutions of Higher Education.

Lovitts, B.E. 2001. *Leaving the ivory tower: The causes and consequences of departure from doctoral study.* Lanham, MD: Rowman & Littlefield.

Marincovich, M., J. Prostco, and F. Stout, eds. 1998. *The professional development of graduate teaching assistants.* Bolton, MA: Anker Publishing Company.

McKeachie, W.J. 1999. *Teaching tips* (10th edition). Boston: Houghton Mifflin Company.

Menges, R.J., M. Weimer, and Associates. 1996. *Teaching on solid ground: Using scholarship to improve practice.* San Francisco: Jossey-Bass.

Millis, B. 2002. Focus group discussion at the Annual Meeting of the Association of American Colleges and Universities. Washington, DC.

Morey, A., 2001. *California's projected need for new faculty: Opportunities and challenges for higher education.* San Diego, CA: Center for Educational Leadership, Innovation and Policy at San Diego State University.

Murray, B. 2000. The growth of the new Ph.D. *Monitor on Psychology.* 31, 24-27.

National Association of Graduate and Professional Students. 2001. Preliminary executive summary of the National Doctoral Program Survey. Washington, DC. http://survey.nagaps.org

National Communications Association. 2001. Preparing future faculty in communication brochure.

National Science Foundation. 2000. *Land of plenty: Diversity in America's competitive edge in science, engineering and technology.* Arlington, VA: National Science Foundation.

Nerad, M. and J. Cerney. 1999. From rumors to facts: Career outcomes of English Ph.D.s. *Communicator* 32:7.

Nyquist, J.D., A.E. Austin, J. Sprague, and D.H. Wulff. 2001. *The development of graduate students as teaching scholars: A four-year longitudinal study.* Center for Instructional Development and Research. Seattle, WA: University of Washington.

Pascarella, E.T. and P.T. Terenzini. 1991. *How college affects students.* San Francisco: Jossey-Bass.

Pruitt-Logan, A.S., J.G. Gaff, and J.E. Jentoft. 2002. *Preparing future faculty in the sciences and mathematics: a guide for change.* Washington, DC: Council of Graduate Schools and the Association of American Colleges and Universities.

Pruitt-Logan, A.S., J.G. Gaff, and R.A. Weibl. 1998. *The impact: Assessing experiences of participants in the Preparing Future Faculty program, 1994-1996.* Preparing Future Faculty Occasional Paper Number 6. Washington, DC: Association of American Colleges and Universities.

Rice, R.E., M.D. Sorcinelli, and A.E. Austin. 2000. *Heeding new voices: Academic careers for a new generation.* New Pathways Working Papers Series #7. Washington, DC: American Association for Higher Education.

Rojas, J.I. 2002. "A graduate student's reflections on training and career issues: recruiting future faculty in psychology." SAPAGA Newsletter, Spring 14, 2.

Sorcinelli, M.D. and C.A. Trower. 2001. Paradise lost: How the academy converts enthusiastic recruits into early-career doubters. Presentation at AAHE Conference on Faculty Roles and Rewards. Tampa, Florida.

Sub-Committee on Directors of Graduate Education. 1998. *What do directors of graduate education do?* Washington, DC: American Sociological Association.

Thomas, V.G. 2002. *Evaluation report of "Shaping the preparation of science and mathematics faculty" project.* Washington, DC: Council of Graduate Schools and Association of American Colleges and Universities.

Turner, C. 2002. *Diversifying the faculty—A guidebook for search committees.* Washington, DC: Association of American Colleges & Universities.

## Web References*

American Political Science Association (APSA), Rostering Program: <www.apsanet.org/about/chairs/rostering.cfm>

American Political Science Association (APSA), Registration Program:<www.apsanet.org/about/chairs/registration.cfm>

Education Trust:

National Science Foundation (NSF) National Science Board, Science and Engineering Indicators, 2002: <http://www.nsf.gov/sbe/srs/seind02/>

Preparing Future Faculty (PFF): <www.preparing-faculty.org>

University of Washington, Re-envisioning the Ph.D. Project: <http://www.grad.washington.edu/envision/>

Woodrow Wilson National Fellowship Foundation (WWNFF), Responsive PhD Initiative: <http://www.woodrow.org/responsivephd/>

*All URLs retrieved on February 25, 2003.